I'D RATHER BE BLIND

The night
hides a world
but reveals
a universe.

I'D RATHER BE BLIND

My life after
Afghanistan.

Grant Lock

broad continent

Melbourne

First published in 2016
Copyright © Grant Lock 2016
The moral right of the author has been asserted.
All rights reserved. No part of this book may be reproduced or transmitted in any form or by any means, electronic or mechanical, including photocopying, recording or by any information storage and retrieval system, without prior written permission from the publisher.

grantlock@shootmefirst.com

Broad Continent Publishing
PO Box 198, Forest Hill Victoria 3131, Australia
management@broadcontinent.com.au
www.broadcontinent.com.au

National Library of Australia Cataloguing-in-Publication entry
Creator: Lock, Grant.
Title: I'd rather be blind : the night hides a world but reveals a universe : my life after Afghanistan /Grant Lock.
ISBN: 978-0-9805264-8-6 (paperback)
Subjects: Lock, Grant.
    Lock, Grant—Family.
    Community development personnel—Australia—Biography.
    People with visual disabilities—Australia—Biography.
    Post-traumatic stress disorder.
    Cultural awareness.
    Pakistan—Social life and customs.
    Afghanistan—Social life and customs.
Dewey Number: 361.7092

Cover photograph by Sam Roberts
sam@samrobertsphotography.com.au
www.samrobertsphotography.com.au
Telephone +61 415 179 717

Photos on pages 30 and 116 by Heather Bellamy. Photo on page 168 by Angela Seewald. All other photos Grant and Janna Lock collection.

Edited by Owen Salter
Designed by Michael Collie
Set in 11 point Minion

Thank you Janna Maxine.
Your love makes possible
the impossible.

ACKNOWLEDGMENTS

> The night hides a world,
> but reveals a universe.
>
> PERSIAN PROVERB

To my companions on my journey into night, thank you for your support and encouragement.

Janna, my amazing fellow-traveller, thank you for your love, friendship and advice. Thank you for all you have given to the concerns, passions and story we share.

Michael Collie, thanks for being my publisher. We have developed a special working relationship. Your energy, vision, professionalism and creative skills have again brought it all together. And thank you Elspeth for being there.

For you blokes at the Blokes' Breakfast: you read, listen and continually encourage me. Len Woodley, for your mentoring, and Bill Hague for your early editing.

Owen Salter, thanks for your masterful final editing.

Thank you, Sam Roberts. Your front cover photography is admired by many.

Thank you, Dosty (Friendly), for your furry, late-night lap-company—even though you make it harder to use the keyboard. You have truly lived up to your name.

For security reasons some names have been changed.

Finally, whether you are sighted, vision impaired, or totally blind, here is good advice:

> Go as far as you can see.
> When you get there
> you'll see further.
>
> PERSIAN PROVERB

CONTENTS

1	Blasphemers will die	13
2	The salesman	15
3	In love with the garbage man	19
4	Macular wall	23
5	Widow of the curly comeback	27
6	The fur piano	31
7	Frishta goes shopping	35
8	Hanging out	39
9	The gun	41
10	The road not travelled	45
11	Some of your children will die	49
12	Survival at Sandspit	51
13	Who?	57
14	The Lamborghini and the big stick	61
15	Road therapy	65
16	Holding on	67
17	Lost	71
18	Flowers and phones	75
19	The plainclothes policeman of Kabul	79
20	Mobile Mo	83
21	The commander and the flood	85
22	Liars, twisters and fools	89
23	Young Lawrence of Arabia	91
24	Double dilemma	95

25	Out of your brain	97
26	The package	103
27	The man	107
28	The delivery	111
29	The Basant trap	113
30	Sadiq Sahib	117
31	Cat and mouse	121
32	Silent night	125
33	Will the real Islam please stand up?	129
34	The club	133
35	The last straw	137
36	And one thing more	141
37	Land-locked Afghanistan	147
38	Stop picking on us!	149
39	Melons	153
40	The fifth face	159
41	Never say never	161
42	That woman	165
43	Miscalculation 1	169
44	The pervert	171
45	Miscalculation 2	175
46	Fumes	179
47	Welcomely obscene	181
48	Flashman	183
49	The rifle	187
50	And the winner is …	193
51	The touch	197
52	The squatters	199
53	When the planets align	203

54	Healing	207
55	The last Wali, the Mad Mullah and Malala	215
56	Julietta	223
57	Tsunami	227
58	The left side	229
59	Finding the mastermind	231
60	Two dollars' worth	237
61	The crab girl	241
62	Hubble images	245
63	The muddy morgue	249
64	Faces of death	251
65	Keemia	255
66	The Afghan wedding and the drummer from hell	257
67	The cigarette	261
68	Grounded	265
69	Flotsam	267

ONE

BLASPHEMERS WILL DIE

ADELAIDE, JULY 2014

I lie here like a broken brick. My phone slips from my fingers.
It was two hours after midnight when Maria rang.
"Dad, I know it's late, but I just saw it on the BBC News website. Two foreign aid workers gunned down in Afghanistan."
My deep-sleep speech is slurry but my brain is clear. "Who, Maria? Who?"
"Two females. No names yet."
"Did they say where?"
"It was in Herat. Didn't you have a project out there?"
"Yes. Our primary mental health care program." My throat tightens. "Run by women. Amazing women."
There is a pause. "Sorry, Dad. I'll ring if I find out more."
The phone clicks. I slump back onto my pillow. A voice in my head is insistent. *It is them. It is them.*
Like the shutters that roll down in Kabul's bazaars at closing time, a wave of weakness sweeps down my body. My breathing is short and shallow. Somehow, I know the voice is right.
I see their faces. I recall their love for serving the people. Now their bodies lie in some Afghan morgue, or more likely the back room of a grotty hospital. Muslims bury their dead on the same day so there is no need for refrigeration. But these two bullet-ridden bodies need to get back to Finland. That's their home, the land of the reindeer and countless lakes.
It's not fair! It's not right!

*

It was just another shopping trip. Old taxi. Afghan bazaar. But during Ramzan, the month of the fast, it's different. The mornings are busy and the afternoons are quiet. The best way to make it through to sundown is to have a long sleep after the lunch you don't have.

Doesn't Allah give a special blessing, and forgive manifold sins, if nothing passes your lips during daylight hours? And isn't there a great blessing for the brave jihadi warriors who eliminate unbelieving *kafirs*, those who call Allah "Father"? That is *shirk*—blasphemy. And how much greater the blessing if the deed is done during the holy month!

Two men have spotted the car. It's the taxi the foreign women usually use. This is going to be easy. The heavenly virgins will not be greeting these brave Taliban fighters today; because they will not meet a martyr's death. Only the blasphemers will die. It will be like shooting fish in a barrel—a rusty yellow barrel with wheels and grimy windows. The well-covered fish are in the back seat.

Amidst the weaving traffic of Herat's Shar-e Naw, a motorbike with a pillion passenger draws alongside the taxi. That's not unusual. Some bikes carry a whole family, so what is another motorbike with a couple of men? The bike holds its position then moves closer. The pillion rider raises an automatic weapon.

Glass shatters. Metal perforates. Souls leave bodies.

TWO

THE SALESMAN

ADELAIDE, 2015

I've always been wary of a balding man with a moustache.
"This will take you places you never thought you could go." He strokes the tips of his moustache. He's sized me up and knows why I'm here. His retail radar has detected that I'm close to making a decision.
Everyone knows we have seasons in our lives. Seasons of change and seasons of self-examination. When I was a young bloke, nothing could stop me. I'd take on anything. And I didn't care what people thought. But these days I'm more sensitive.
"Seems to be losing his confidence."
"Can't make quick decisions any more."
"Not moving like he used to."
Then one night I am lying there, and my wife sighs and says, "Don't worry, dear, I guess it doesn't matter if you can't do what you used to do."
It all hurts.
But this morning, I finally got things into perspective. I looked in the mirror. I didn't see the guy I used to see. I have to be realistic: my self-confidence has slipped and I need a bit of help. Not from those mollifying counsellors with all their jargon and endless appointments. No, I need something tangible, something that puts real power into my hands.
That's when I made my decision. And that's why I'm here in this city showroom.
Don't get me wrong. It's not entirely an age thing. I figure the Grim Reaper is still well down the track for me. But sometimes you just have to do what you have to do.
"Any colour other than white?" I ask.
"Not in this model, sir. But you can have coloured trim"—he strokes the cuff of my pale blue shirt—"to match your favourite outfit. The choice is yours. Bronze, aqua, silver. Whatever. Anything goes these

days!" He smiles. "Just last week a woman from Burnside took one of these. She is so pleased. A big step, but it's changed her life. People notice her. Her self-esteem has risen enormously."

This guy sure knows how to press the buttons. But he's right. People do need to pay me a bit more attention. I'll no longer be just another sheep in the crowd.

"It's the latest model, sir, and just right for you." Adam doesn't seem the right name for a bald guy with a small moustache, but no matter. Normal is over for me, and he knows it. "Step over here and I'll show you how it folds down." He starts the demonstration and adds quietly, "You get maximum attention when it's down."

I smile. I'm impressed. I can already see the heads turning when I arrive at the Morialta Gorge car park, or turn up at the gym.

Adam turns to me. "Why don't you take it out for a test run?"

He doesn't need to offer a second time. I can't wait to get out onto the street. Now I'll get the respect and attention I deserve. After all, not many people own one of these. Not even my identical twin brother, although I know he's thinking seriously about it. And I wonder what my mother would think if she could see me now. Would she be proud or disappointed?

Adam knows what I want to hear. "People will stop and look at you when you go by," he chuckles. "It's pure power, sir."

I don't need convincing. But I want to be sure of the options. "Are there any other models?"

"Of course," he says and waves his hand around the show room. "It's your choice. You don't have to take the latest release."

But I'm hooked. I feel its profile. Nice! Secretly, I can't wait to leave the showroom to try out my new people impresser.

"Just here," Adam says. I sign and head for the door. I can feel the eyes of the young receptionist following me. "All the best, sir," she says in a sweet voice.

"Thank you." I pause and give her half a nod and a satisfied smile. As I turn to leave, I collide with a large woman entering with a guide dog. "Watch it!" I blurt out. I repent immediately. "I beg your pardon, ma'am. I'm very sorry." She doesn't reply but forges ahead, resolutely gripping the frame on her black Labrador.

Clearly it wasn't her fault. She's probably totally blind. I'm really glad I don't need a guide dog—not yet, anyway. I still have a bit of peripheral vision left, and this new white cane will make all the difference.

※

The salesman was right. I am noticed now. When I cross the road nobody assumes I'm on drugs. They see the cane and slow down. They even stop for me. That's power, real power. Now, wherever I go, my white cane goes with me. It has become my good friend. But I'd readily trade it for the driver's licence I so reluctantly surrendered when I returned from Afghanistan.

May Kabul be without gold,
but never without snow.
AFGHAN PROVERB

THREE

IN LOVE WITH THE GARBAGE MAN

ADELAIDE, 2015

She must have better hearing than I do. On Monday mornings, long before I pick up the roar of the council truck, I feel Janna stirring beside me. As the "stop–start" of the big diesel approaches, she is sitting up and peering through our bedroom window.

Once she even ran out in her skimpy summer nightie and gave him a little box, gift-wrapped and tied with red ribbon. Christmas was the excuse. My vision is going, but through the window I saw enough. I groaned, pulled the blanket up around my head and hoped the neighbours were still counting sheep.

It's not that she is stuck on one particular guy. It seems she has a thing for all council drivers. Parcel delivery drivers don't move her. The cheerful postie is ignored. The young muscle man who delivers building supplies over the road doesn't even score a glance. But when Monday morning comes around, guess who is all bright-eyed, waiting for her hero to appear?

Unlike my wife, this average mortal is a slow starter on Monday mornings. After a full weekend, I covet all the sleep I can get. At my desk, time snails down to slow motion. The voice of my ZoomText screen-reader drones faintly. It's only multiple shots of dark chocolate mocha that enable me to reach the moving mirage of my lunch break.

The mechanical arm thrusts the bins up and down.
Thump, pause, thump.
Roars forward.
Thump, pause, thump.
Roars forward.

As the noise grows louder, I hear her enchanted sigh. "I love that man."

I had always thought that phrase was reserved for me. We sleep between the same sheets, but right now, I know where her thoughts are.

※

She's back in Kabul, Afghanistan, holding the corner of her long *chaddar* shawl to her nose as she hurries past the accumulating, buzzing mound at the end of our street. The locals empty everything onto it.

The first to check it out are the kids. Bottles, tins and paper all help put a piece of flat bread on the family table. And if there is a portion of unconsumed bread or discarded rice in the trash, well, that's a bonus. Then come the stray dogs. Even the fat-tailed sheep have a nibble as their bearded shepherds lead them out to rocky pastures. But the permanent custodians, along with their grave-filling diseases, are the flies. No wonder Afghanistan has one of the world's highest child mortality rates.

With a bit of luck, and some persuasive currency from the neighbours, a municipal truck will pull up once every seven or eight weeks. There's a flurry of shovels and we start all over again. In only a fortnight vehicles and pedestrians will have to veer to avoid the creeping mass.

It didn't help to learn that Kabul was labelled the capital city with the highest level of atmospheric faecal material. Not surprising when so much is mixed up, stirred up and shovelled out onto those dusty roads. Our organisation was changing that. We trained the locals to build effective toilets. Similar, but superior, to the long drop we had on the farm when I was a kid.

But the Afghan winters change everything. The old white-beards have a proverb: *"Kabul bey zar barsh, bey barf ney*—May Kabul be without gold, but never without snow." Without snow crops will wither in the fields and wells in the city will dry up. Janna and I loved the snow. Its forgiving, pristine blanket covered the sanitary iniquities of a battered and bruised population. It was a welcome change from the blistering heat we endured for twenty years on the plains of Pakistan.

※

That's why, for my wife, Mondays are special. And that's why the sweet roar of that diesel truck pumps a surge of gratitude through her veins. And it's why she loves every driver the local council sends our way.

"It's not *just* the drivers," I remonstrate with her. "There are lots of other people taking care of the business. In the offices, the landfill sites, the recycling stations ... lots of people. It's not *just* the drivers."

She doesn't even hear me. She's sitting up in bed, peering out the window.

"I love that man."

FOUR

MACULAR WALL

ADELAIDE, 2015

After the meeting
it's time for tea,
mix and match,
laugh and chat.
But as for me
I'm out of community.

Dysfunction at the junction
where personality and disability
meet gut-level grief and pain.
I peer at you,
my faceless friends,
in vain.

There's a fuzzy wall
between me and you.
Lonely corner,
bitter pie.
No Jack. No Horner.
Alone am I.

Fractured molecule
in a seemingly functional cell,
unneeded,
useless,
redundant.
Macular slice of separation.
The taste of hell.

Leper.
"Unclean. Unclean.
Can't you hear my bell
ringing out the warning?"
Yet pleading for your touch,
your voice,
your association.

Surely that's not too much to ask!
But here I float,
below the bastions of your castle,
melting iceberg in a lonely moat.

And in this opaque corner,
marginalised by the unseeing focus
of my muddy eyes,
internally I scream,
"Where are you, Jack?
"Where are you, Horner?"

Mrs Glibly passes by.
"Er, who are you?"
I tentatively ask.
Glibly she replies,
"But Grant! You know *me!*
You know *my* voice!"
And glibly
she swans into the night.

But I have no choice,
if I can't make the connection right.
I'm lost,
alone,
out in the cold.
Old Jack Frost.

Then *you* come,
out of the audio forest,
a welcome, blurry tree.
I feel your touch,
I hear my name.
You say, "Grant, come and join us.
Come with me!"

Thank you.
You are beautiful.

FIVE

WIDOW OF THE CURLY COMEBACK

CRYSTAL BROOK, 18 APRIL 1922

I never met Grandpa Steve, and I never received any tennis tips from him. The Curly Comeback made the racquet look like a toy. He was the best tennis player in the northern Flinders Ranges. On Saturday nights, he would trade his racquet for a violin bow and add zest to the Beltana bush dances. With a rugged complexion and shock of curly hair, he cut a handsome figure. That's what the photos portray.

※

Steve and Willy set out early with Old Napoleon at the front of the wagon team. The powerful draught horse is a trusted friend. Steve couldn't bear to leave him behind at Puttapa Station when the unforgiving trinity of low wool prices, rabbits and the bank manager squeezed them off the property. The other three horses are inexperienced and only just learning to work together. Old Napoleon is the stabiliser, the equine glue that holds the new team together.

Five miles later they reach H. Taylor's big merchandise shed in Crystal Brook. The autumn blue sky is being replaced by a rolling bank of dark cloud. Steve peers at the horizon. "Storm's coming in, son." He leaps from the wagon. "Better get this stuff loaded quick. Gotta stop at the store to get a little surprise for your mum. And some tennis balls." He grins. "This could be the break of the season."

Darkening sky. Swirling leaves. Pungent smell of rain on parched earth.

The horses are getting restless.

At last, all the timber and corrugated iron is stacked on the wagon. The Curly Comeback springs to the ground, unties the lead horse from the hitching rail and is about to vault back onto the wagon.

There is only one bolt of lightning. There's no time lag between the flash and the thunder. It strikes H. Taylor's shed. The explosion reverberates around the cavernous structure like the opening salvo of an artillery barrage at the Somme.

With raw terror the three new horses charge forward. The explosion is even too much for Old Napoleon and he joins the stampede. Steve leaps at the bridle of the bolting leader. Surely, if he can restrain Old Napoleon, he'll hold the team! But the great stockman can't steady them. Three tons of pounding horse-flesh hurtle forward unencumbered by the loaded wagon.

"Jump for it, Willy!" Steve shouts to his eleven-year old son. The Curly Comeback tenaciously holds on and the bit bites deep, but the old leader feels nothing. Loose fencing wire snags Steve's dancing feet. He stumbles and falls. Heavy wagon wheels are right behind.

My father watched as his father's body was carried off in the rain. He never ever spoke to me about what happened that day. When I was eleven, I helped him to pour a tennis court on the family farm, two hundred miles from Taylor's yard.

One lightning bolt changed everything. Steve and Elisabeth and the four children had just taken possession of Wattle Brae, a small property at Huddleston near Crystal Brook. Huddleston has a railway siding, a store, a church and, yes, a tennis court. They had mortgaged everything to make a fresh start. Now Steve is gone.

It's just not possible for the new widow to run the new property on her own. The two girls could help, but both boys are still in primary school.

"Pity," the locals commiserate.

"She'll have to sell up."

"Only thing she can do."

But they don't reckon on the iron character of God-fearing Elisabeth. And it all happens on her birthday. She is forty-two.

Nice birthday present, Lord. Here I am with no husband, a new farm, five mouths to feed, the bank payments to meet, a crop to put in and no one to work the land.

The young mother of four is no newcomer to struggle. She lost her own mother when she was six. Elisabeth was tough. She had to be.

❊

Billy lays down his swag and knocks on the door of the spartan farmhouse. "The neighbours tell me you could use some help, Missus," he says with an unusual drawl.

He's soon sitting at the well-scrubbed kitchen table, quaffing tea and complimenting Elisabeth on her freshly baked bread.

"I can only pay you till the crop is in, Mr Smith, but I'd be grateful for your help," says Elisabeth, and an agreement is reached.

Every morning before dawn, Billy is up cutting chaff and doling out oats to stoke the metabolic furnaces of Old Napoleon and the other horses. Then, after an equally hearty breakfast, he leads the harnessed team to the field. Lizzie and the kids milk the cows and churn the butter. Then the boys head off to school.

Finally, the wheat crop is in.

"I'd really like to keep you on, Mr Smith," the widow says, "but I thank you for your service to me and the children."

The muscular farmhand shoulders his swag. "You're welcome, Missus." He disappears down the track. Grateful Elisabeth watches him go and gives thanks for dark-haired Billy Smith, the Aboriginal saviour of Wattle Brae.

The wound of the sword will heal,
but not that of the tongue.
AFGHAN PROVERB

SIX

THE FUR PIANO

CRYSTAL BROOK, 1937

Old Napoleon pulled and pulled for Elisabeth for another three years, till his heart wore out and he collapsed in the harness. The fatherless family continued to arm-wrestle fate and fluctuating seasons. My dad, and then his brother Ben, left school early. Gradually the tide turned. The bank was repaid, and they took a smaller loan to buy a crawler tractor.

※

Elisabeth Lock walks across the paddock to visit another widow. Like Billy, the saviour of Wattle Brae, the older woman's name is Smith. Hers was a childless marriage, and now Elisabeth and her sons share-farm her holding.

The white-haired neighbour takes a break from her baking and prepares a pot of tea. "Your boys have grown into fine young men, Lizzie. They're doing a good job with my property."

The younger woman nods in appreciation.

Mrs Smith carefully lays out her English porcelain tea set. "What I want to know, Lizzie, is why you ever left the sheep station up north. Wool was making a lot of money, and the seasons were good back then."

A shadow drifts over Elisabeth's work-worn features. "The seasons and the prices did come good, Mrs Smith—but only after we left." She raises a freshly buttered scone halfway to her mouth. "If only we could have hung on for another year, we could have handled the drought and the dingoes." She gazes out of her neighbour's kitchen window. "But it was the rabbits that drove us out."

The Locks, like so many early settlers in South Australia, found work and sustenance in the rugged Flinders Ranges. Some were shepherds; others were miners, shearers or teamsters. And some helped breed and break in Thomas Elder's imported Afghan camels.

Mrs Smith starts to knead the dough for another batch of scones. "I've never heard of your Puttapa, Lizzie."

"It's a small station near Beltana, right next to Sliding Rock."

"Ah yes, I remember the Sliding Rock mine. The copper boom lasted for twenty years."

Elisabeth butters another scone. "Steve was a great manager for other people. But he always wanted to run his own sheep station. So he started looking around. Balcanoona was up for sale, and he rode around the Gammon Ranges to have a look." Her voice quietens. "He nearly died out there."

"Nearly died?"

"There was this two-day dust storm and he lost his bearings. Ran out of water. He and his horse had just about had it. And there I was, stuck back at Old Nilpena with number three on the way, wondering what had happened to him. Thank the Lord for the birds—they knew where the springs were and he followed them."

Mrs Smith has shuffled to the wood box and is standing in the middle of the kitchen with a log in her hand. "Oh, Lizzie," she whispers. She tosses the wood in the stove and wipes her hands on her apron. "But you bought Puttapa instead?"

"It was the spring of 1911, not long after Bill was born. Steve was so enthusiastic. Of course there was no stock on the place, he went straight off and bought a thousand sheep, and some really good rams. He dreamed of producing the best wool in the Flinders." Lizzie's voice falters, "But it turned into a nightmare. Thanks to the dingoes."

Mrs Smith slips the tray of scones into the oven and steps back. "Dingoes?"

"Steve yarded the sheep every night. But that didn't stop them. One night they got into the yards, and ripped into the mob. The yard-fence must have given away. Next morning there were dead and maimed sheep everywhere. Have you ever seen what a pack of those wild dogs can do, Mrs Smith."

The stooped scone-maker slowly shakes her head.

"They don't just kill to eat. They go berserk. It's all a big game. They tear at the throat, the flank, the belly, of anything they can run down.

There were disembowelled sheep everywhere. Steve had to put scores of them out of their misery."

"Oh dear! I'm glad we don't have dingoes down here, not since they built the dog-proof fence."

"Steve was livid and vowed to clean out the dingoes, or at least to get the numbers down before the lambing season started. He even pulled out of playing tennis. For a while it was all traps, strychnine baits and rifles. I shot a few myself when they came snooping round the homestead. Then, just when we were getting on top of the wild dogs, the rabbits came, and we had to start over again."

"Too many for the dingoes?"

Elisabeth laughs. "They were so full of rabbit! At least that meant they didn't worry the lambs too much." Her jaws tighten. "Rabbits! We hated the sight of those flop-eared invaders. They were everywhere. They ate every skerrick of sheep feed, and in summer they came to the springs in droves. We built trap fences around the waters and sometimes we'd get over a thousand in one day. Steve would wring their necks, and I'd help skin them. The kids would cart the carcasses away so they didn't foul up the springs."

She laughs again. "Too bad the Sliding Rock mine closed down. I could have sold a lot of rabbit pies to those miners!"

"Any money in the skins, Lizzie?"

"We used to sell the pelts for nine pence a pound—went into felt hats, I guess." She grins. "At least I got a piano out of it. I'd always wanted my own piano. A ton of rabbit fur got me a steel-framed Beale. Then I started teaching the kids." She straightens her back a little. "Nellie is a paid music teacher these days." She pauses to sip her tea. "And Steve used to practise his violin with me. You never knew when someone would gallop out from Beltana to get him to play for a dance, or a wedding. That brought in a few bob too. And I put away a bit from teaching the kids on the station next door."

She sniffs the air. "I reckon your scones are about done, Mrs Smith. It was a really solid piano, you know. Handled the heat and dust pretty well. After those big dust storms, we had to shovel the stuff out."

The aroma of freshly baked scones fills the room. The older widow straightens her stooped frame and looks squarely at her visitor. "You sure have done it tough." She hands over a basket. "These might come in handy when the boys get off that noisy tractor. And Lizzie, I'm glad you're at Wattle Brae. I'm glad you're my neighbour."

As Elisabeth dons her coat and scarf, Mrs Smith raises her voice a little. "How are things going with Bill and that young lady over at Gladstone?"

"We'll see," Lizzie smiles. "He seems to head over there whenever he can."

Warmed by her old neighbour's kindness, fifty-seven-year-old Lizzie returns home across the field, pondering the future. Some people are natural strategists and Elisabeth Lock is one of them.

Yes, Bill, you're on to a good thing with that Muriel Hamp. I like her. She's intelligent and friendly, and, from what I hear, she's not afraid of hard work. Sings in the church choir and plays a handy game of tennis too. Bet she can't use either hand though, like I used to. That sure confused those Beltana ladies!

Halfway across the paddock she stoops to pull out a solitary horehound weed. In the distance she can hear the new crawler tractor, churning and chugging in front of the plough.

You're right, Mrs Smith. That thing does make a terrible noise. But at least we don't have to cut a paddock of hay to feed it when it's not working. We'll need more paddocks when both boys get married. Just as well they don't know about my secret bank account or they'd want it to buy some fancy farm machine. There's a lot of butter and egg money in that account, and piano lesson money, too. One day, we just might need it to help buy another farm.

※

My parents, Bill and Muriel, married in the autumn of 1939, just a few months before Hitler marched into Poland. The following year my sister Gaynor arrived, then my twin brother Barry and I. In 1947 we all moved 180 miles west to Kimbolton, a good farm six miles west of Kimba on the Eyre Peninsula. And yes, it was Grandma Elisabeth's secret bank account that made it possible.

SEVEN

FRISHTA GOES SHOPPING

ADELAIDE, 2015

I hear the roller door of our garage opening. I stride from my office, switch on the electric kettle, and before Janna has turned off the car, I am waiting to carry the grocery bags into the kitchen.

"Was it busy in the shops today?"

She ignores my question. "I met such a lovely lady," she says. "Make the tea and I'll tell you. I'll put the things away later."

She heads for her favourite armchair, but she doesn't lean back into it. "She was so pleased to see me."

"So who is the mystery woman?" I say as I overfill a mug. These days I always sit the mugs and cups in the sink so there isn't any mess when I miscalculate. "She's a Muslim?" It's more a statement than a question. When my wife is excited like this, I already know who she has met. And I am a bit envious.

It is easy for Aussie women to notice and relate to Muslim women because of their distinctive Islamic dress. Of course we men notice them too. Even vision-impaired blokes like me stand a good chance of seeing enough of their outfits to make the identification.

But then, for me, comes the big struggle. Where I've worked for twenty-four years, men—at least, respectable men—do not look directly at women. You learn to avert your gaze. You shake hands with the men and give them a greeting hug and a cheek-to-cheek kind of kiss. It's the cultural thing to do. But unless you are very close friends with the family, you don't look at or speak to the women.

So it's major reverse culture shock when you get off the plane in Australia and the women here want to give you a hug and a kiss. Your body goes tense and your confused mind shouts, "Hey, that's not right!" And when you embrace Aussie guys, you feel their bodies stiffen, and it is *their* minds that are shouting, "Hey, that's not right!"

For us blokes, it is much harder to identify Muslim men because most of them wear what we wear. I suppose the answer is to be friendly to everyone. But I especially want to be friendly with Muslim men. It's easy to identify them when they are accompanied by their head-covered women. Then I can look them in the eye and start with a "Hello" or a "G'day". Of course, they get an extra buzz if I say, *"As salaam alekoom"*, which simply means, "Peace be with you." You can't get a better greeting than that. And the reply, *"Vaalekoom salaam"*, just means, "And also with you."

I set the mug of English Breakfast tea next to Janna. "Where did you meet her?"

"It wasn't just her. She had two teenage boys with her. I passed them in the Marion Mall and I could tell from their faces they were Hazara. She wore a long skirt and underneath I could see the traditional loose *tombon* trousers with the lace trim. And she had a navy blue cardigan, and a white *chaddar* shawl over her head. She wasn't wealthy—I could tell from the quality of the cloth. She had such a friendly round face." Janna sips her tea. "She looked a bit lost."

"That's understandable."

"Well, not lost exactly. A bit uncertain."

"If they're Hazara," I comment, "who knows what they have been through."

Not everyone knows that in Afghanistan the Hazaras are treated as "bottom of the barrel" people. Their name comes from the word *hazar,* which means "thousand". Eight hundred years ago, Genghis Khan's fast-moving army was organised in companies of one thousand. Those who were left to control the defeated Afghans married local women. The Hazaras have been easy targets for the Taliban, who just look for their slightly slanted Mongolian eyes.

"And …?" I ask.

"I put my shopping list back in my bag and followed them into Big W. They'd stopped at the jeans rack, and the boys were choosing while she held the jeans up against them. I said, *'As salaam alekoom'* and they automatically responded, *'Vaalekoom salaam.'* Their eyes popped a bit when they realised it was an Aussie greeting them."

"*'Shumar Hazara asteen?'* I asked her, 'Are you Hazara?'

"She nodded, *'Ballay. Ballay.'* Then her face switched on with such a warm smile. I guess she was so pleased to be greeted in a language she could comprehend."

"'*Khoosh armdeed*,' I said, 'Welcome.' And I gave her the regular hug and three kisses. She just clung to me. Finally she let me go, and I could see she had tears in her eyes. I told her that I used to live in her country. Then she absolutely beamed, and gave me another big hug."

Janna is quiet for a moment, then she whispers, "It was so special."

"And where were they from?"

"One of the boys said they come from Ghazni. I think I must have switched back to English; I've forgotten so much of my Dari. But both boys could understand me, and they've only been here four months. I hope I bump into them again. It really made her day."

"And yours, Frishta," I say, using the name the widows gave her in Kabul. It means "Angel".

She smiles. "It makes such a difference when people are made welcome."

I nod.

I think of Anwar. Anwar is from Pakistan, and when I am in the city, we have a coffee before he starts work. He's a hard-working young man, and over the years I have seen his confidence grow. He will soon be able to apply for citizenship.

And our Iranian friends, Mazool and Safina, are doing well, too. Their children are at high school and their enthusiasm is infectious. They will be a real asset to our Australian community. "We love it here," Mazool said when they came around last time. "We are not being watched. There is so much freedom." Safina smiles. She understands a lot more English than she can speak.

I am amazed that it is only a year since I met this cheerful Tehrani taxi driver. There was so much talking going on in the taxi that we neglected to exchange addresses. I rang the taxi company. "Yes," the girl said, "we have a record of the trip, but we're not allowed to give the driver's details. Give us your number and, if he wants to, he can ring you." Within half an hour Mazool's excited voice came down the phone, and that was the start of our family friendship.

EIGHT

HANGING OUT

ADELAIDE, 2015

Yes, you never know where or when you can show friendship. It could just be a welcoming smile or a greeting—or it may be a more extended relationship. But it's not likely to happen for me in shopping malls because these days I am seldom there.

There was a time when I could help Janna in the supermarket. I could find things and bring them back to the trolley. Now I can't focus enough to do even that. These days, the best thing about those big shops is the music they play. It makes me want to dance. But I lose concentration and don't keep up with Janna. It's not a happy moment when she turns with an armful of toilet rolls or packets of milk and I am not there with the trolley.

"Let's face it, Grant," she said finally, "you are not an asset when I'm shopping. Better I do it myself. You can spray the fertiliser on the garden, vacuum the carpet or hang out the washing. At least that way you're being useful."

She is right. This kind of job division seems to work better than my trying to do slow rock with a shopping trolley in a busy supermarket.

When it comes to hanging out the washing, I definitely like bath towels. Not too small and fiddly. Not too big and blowy, like those confusing double bed sheets. Towels are quick and straightforward, and they empty the washing basket fast. For a vision impaired person that's very fulfilling. But then there are all those little things at the bottom: socks, underwear, handkerchiefs and tea-towels. Just when you think you're making good progress and will get back inside to see the midday news, you hit that small stuff and you don't even get back in time for the weather.

To date, I have never had Janna come along and correct my towel hanging. Not so for other things. She unclips this and realigns that, along with lots of helpful, but wasted, advice. "What is it about men hanging out clothes?" she moans as she readjusts the garments.

I wave my hands at the sky. "Hey, it's a windy day. It doesn't matter how you hang them, they'll all be dry in an hour."

"That's not the point," she says.

Well, what is the point, I silently argue. *You hang out the clothes to dry them, don't you? And if it's a great drying day, just hang them out and let the air do its work. What could be simpler than that?*

This is one of the times I am thankful my central vision is not working, because I don't have to wither under the 'just-do-it-properly-Grant' gaze.

She straightens her underwear, and then she gets to the socks. "Grant, how many times have I told you to put matching socks together? Makes it easier to fold them and put them away." It seems appropriate to remind her about my vision problems. "Don't give me that," she says. "Even before your sight went bad, you didn't do it properly."

I give a sulky mumble. "Doesn't have to be perfectly right to dry."

She stops her readjustment. "What did you say?"

"I sure miss my sight … but I'll try."

NINE

THE GUN

KIRTHAR MOUNTAINS, 1985

It is eighteen months since we arrived to serve the people of the "Land of the Pure". My wife has decided to be known as "Janna". We soon realised that the Sindhi people could not pronounce "Maxine" and, furthermore, it sounded like an undesirable word in their vocabulary.

Right from the start, Janna doesn't feel right about our trip to the barren Kirthar National Park. We haven't driven more than a few dusty miles when she leans my way and whispers, "I'm not comfortable with this, Grant. There's something about that Akhram."

"Pipe down," I whisper back, hoping the rumble of the wheels on the rough road will muffle my voice. "He's sitting right behind us."

But I can feel the tension radiating from her stiff body. I have to admit that my emotional Geiger counter is set pretty low. Is it just because I am an Aussie bloke, or is it that I am genetically thick skinned? If the Geiger counter was operating correctly, it would be ticking violently now, particularly after she leans my way again and hisses, "He's got a gun!"

I grip the wheel more firmly but decide not to overreact. If Akhram turns nasty, we are in a vulnerable position. He is directly behind us in the backseat of our Toyota Hilux, between our two girls.

Janna hisses again, "I can see it in his belt, Grant. Under his coat. Do something!"

"Ok! Ok!" I hiss back.

My brain is spinning. *What can I do? We're in the middle of nowhere. We haven't seen anyone or anything all morning. It looks like a moonscape out here. If I stop and confront him, he could pull that gun on the kids. Best keep calm, drive on and see what develops.*

Janna is thinking otherwise. *Why don't you stop while you can? Turn around! Drive back!*

I set my jaw. *Gotta keep going. Can't upset him.*

Oh, Grant! You are so thick! And so pig-headed!

Angela and Maria detect the radioactivity in the front seat. *What are they arguing about up there? Why are they hissing and snapping at each other?*

Young Matthew, squeezed in beside his mother, doesn't seem to notice. He keeps jabbering on about the fossils the brochure promised.

Janna's eyes demand action. In the rear view mirror I see swarthy Akhram. His coat gapes and the butt of his gun protrudes. Both girls see it too. They stiffen.

"Where do we find the fossils, Mr Akhram?" Matthew pipes up from the front seat.

"*Argay, argay, merah bucha*—Ahead, ahead, my boy."

Janna's brain is racing. *That's right, clever Mr Akhram! Just keep taking us further and further into nowhere, then pull the gun and kidnap us, or maybe just shoot us and steal the Hilux.* Her knuckles are white. *He could do something terrible to the girls.*

She glares at me. *Do something! Before it's too late!*

The adrenalin is pumping, but I decide that the something I will do is to do nothing. If I can engage him a bit, that might help somehow.

"Ah, Akhram Jhi, I see you have a gun. Why is it you need to carry a gun?"

"Protection, Janaab. Many poachers out here. I protect blackbuck, Markhor goat and ibex. Very rare. Must have gun."

That reassures me. Yes, Janna is overreacting. He may not have a ranger's uniform, but if he is the game warden, of course he would need that gun. Those animals are rare and worth a fortune on the black market. I want to think the best of him. It's all part of his job.

I continue the dialogue. "Haven't seen much sign of any blackbuck, Akhram Jhi."

Our guide frowns. "*Muaf karo, Janaab*—Very sorry. They were here last week. *Shaeed argay*—Maybe ahead."

We crawl along the four-wheel drive track for another ten minutes. Janna is rigid. She fossicks in her handbag and a pops small white tablet into her mouth.

Angela is super uptight. This is not the adventure she has been looking forward to.

Suddenly, Akhram leans forward and gives an order. *"Roko! Iddr roko!*—Stop! Stop here!"

I pull up near the crown of a low, bald hill. A plume of powdery dust swirls around us. "No further can go," Akhram declares in broken English. "No more road. *Sarak khuttam*—Road finished!" Then he gestures toward the top of the hill. "Plenty fossils here."

Matthew is out the door like a shot. Angela follows. She has sat beside that gun long enough.

I open my door and join them. Maria sits tight.

Akhram gestures. "Come, girl!"

Maria shakes her head vigorously. There is no way she is getting out with that big man with a gun in his belt. She reaches for her book and refuses to look up. Akhram growls something in Urdu, turns to the closed front door and opens it. "Come, Memsahib."

Janna freezes, then reaches for her embroidery bag. *"Mehribani, Jhi*— No, thanks. I will do my stitching." She pulls the door shut. *Not in a thousand years, mate! And leave my kids alone!*

Black-moustached Akhram is not happy. He opens the door and repeats the invitation. It sounds more like a command. "Come, Memsahib!"

Janna pulls the door shut again, locks it and, with shaking fingers, drags wool from the bag.

His face darkens, but he turns and stalks after the fossickers. I follow. His demeanour is changing, and I don't like it. *But what can I do? He's a big guy. Could I jump him? I doubt it. Keep cool, Grant. He's getting edgy. Better just play along.*

"Look at this, Dad!" Matthew shouts. He runs over with a rock which clearly contains a fossilised crab.

"And I've found a round one!" Angela calls out. "Some ancient sea creature. Wow! I reckon it's an ammonite." Fossil fever has taken her mind off our guide. I compliment him on his choice of location.

He beckons us on. And on.

TEN

THE ROAD NOT TRAVELLED

KIRTHAR MOUNTAINS, 1985

Janna watches us disappear over the stony ridge. *Will I ever see them again? Will I hear the shots?*

She turns to the back seat. "Lock all the doors, Maria!" Then she opens her handbag for the tranquillisers. Sure, normal people are not supposed to need these. But the doctor said she should keep some on hand for emergencies. Emergencies like watching your kids and husband disappear over the hill with an armed man.

Maria pushes the buttons on both back doors, lies down and forces herself to sleep.

Janna waits, and waits. *I could drive off, try to find help ... but Grant has the keys. I could wake Maria and we could run for it. But where? We haven't seen a soul or a vehicle all morning. And this is near the Baluchistan border, and Baluchistan has a reputation for kidnapping. Please, Jesus—not kidnapping! Jesus!*

She repeats the name over and over in her head.

※

This is the Kirthar National Park in the province of Sindh, Pakistan. During the first year of our service we had been without wheels. But now we have the double cab Hilux. Ideal for our desert development work, and ideal to explore parts of the country off the beaten track, like this national park. It is much more remote than the tourist guide book indicated. But, coming from the edge of the Australian outback, remoteness is not new to us,.

"I want to see blackbuck deer, Dad," nine-year-old Matthew had announced. "Did you know they were extinct here, but the Chicago zoo still had them and sent some back as a gift?"

"And the place has lots of fossils," Angela had said as she stabbed a finger at the relevant page of the guide book.

So we made our plans and drove for hours through dusty, flat plains. Countless large lizards poked their orange heads from their holes. In their reptilian way, were they trying to warn us to turn back? If so, we took no notice. We paused at a lonely group of mud houses. A blindfolded camel was going round and round, operating a Persian wheel. I wondered for how many hundreds, even thousands, of years they had been using that device to pull up water for their onion fields. Nothing else was growing. Just onions.

We finally pulled into the deserted Park base and scanned the circle of small accommodation buildings. "We're the only ones here, Grant," Janna whispered. A door opened and a burly ranger appeared. He greeted us in a mixture of Urdu and broken English.

"*Khoosh armdeed*. Velcome, velcome, Sahib! My name Akhram. We are for you to be waiting." Well, at least they were expecting us. No doubt the booking came through the rusty wires we had seen, looping from one twisted pole to another, snaking alongside the track.

Another man appeared. "This, Feroze," said Akhram. "If you need cook, Feroze very good cook." Feroze gave a toothy grin and enthusiastically wiped his grimy hands on a grimier apron.

Akhram led us to one of the half dozen shabby cabins. They were laid out in a half circle. I figured some international conservation group had something to do with this. And there were no walls around them. Even though there was no one else for scores of miles, it didn't seem right. In Pakistan you always have walls.

We looked around. No other vehicles. No other people.

Akhram was keen to make plans. "Tomorrow, Sahib, I show you blackbuck and fossils. We start early. Long drive."

He could see the question in my eyes as I scanned for their vehicle.

"No *ghari* here. No vehicle!" He points his chin at our Hilux. "We use your *ghari*. Leave early. *Sart bajay*."

I was puzzled. How did they manage out here without an on-site vehicle?

Akhram was still talking. "*Sart bajay*, Sahib. Seven o'clock. Oκ?"

I nod.

Over the ridge, Akhram continues to beckon us on, pointing at the ground. Eleven-year-old Angela and her brother need no encouragement. There are regular shouts as they drop interesting rocks into their buckets.

I've almost dismissed the gun thing. He is just doing his job. I reckon Janna's overreacting.

We are moving down the other side of the ridge when Angela shouts again. "Look at this one, Dad!" I look up, and my internal Geiger counter starts clicking furiously. It's all to do with the dirt road. I can see it winding on for miles, toward the distant mountains of Baluchistan.

Hey! Didn't Akhram say there was no more road? But it goes on for miles. Why did he insist there was no way ahead? He said it clearly in English and Urdu. I don't understand.

An unwelcome prophecy sent to us by a well-meaning, albeit eccentric, Aussie oracle comes to mind: *"You will return from Pakistan, but some of your children will die."*

I turn back toward Akhram. He is busy encouraging Matt to go a little further. My muscles tighten. Janna wasn't overreacting at all. That man is way too close to my kids.

To the top of even the highest mountain
there is a path.
AFGHAN PROVERB

ELEVEN

SOME OF YOUR CHILDREN WILL DIE

KIRTHAR MOUNTAINS, 1985

I had long dismissed the prophecy but the words won't leave my head.
Bringing our children to Pakistan had always attracted criticism. "It might be alright for you, but taking your three kids to a place like that is crazy!" But we knew the people of the heaviest-populated desert in the world were waiting for us, and then the people of the northern mountains, and finally the war-weary in Afghanistan. Our kids had lots of adventures, and they all met their future life-partners in a little international school in the foothills of the Himalayas.

Hadn't God called us to serve the people of Pakistan? Janna and I chose to be guided by a letter from a long-term worker in Pakistan. "As for that family, the Locks, they will come to Pakistan and be a great blessing. The people in the desert are waiting for them."

❋

Yet, deep in my being, fear is rising. As I stare at the road that is not supposed to be there, I am desperately hoping that this prophecy will not come true.

I have to keep cool. Act natural. "Ok, kids!" I call out firmly. "Time to go!"

They start to complain. Akhram is out in front and I can feel his indignant glare.

"First, bring your buckets here so I can see what you've found." They mumble their way back. As we lean over their buckets, I speak quietly and urgently. "Listen, kids, don't look up. Mum is right about this guy. He's telling us lies. He clearly said there was no road ahead, but there is."

Their faces go pale.

"I think he's on his way back," Angela whispers. Remorse has replaced her enthusiasm for finding fossils and seeing wildlife.

"Act natural," I say, "but spread out." Then I raise my voice for Akhram's benefit. "Great job, kids. See what you can find on the way back."

※

Janna is scanning the ridge for movement. One head appears. It is Matthew's. Her heart misses a beat. *Has he got Grant and Angela? I heard no shots. Perhaps he has a silencer?*

Angela's head appears, then the two men. *Thank you, Lord.*

I keep Akhram engaged. "Too bad we didn't see the blackbuck, Akhram Jhi. But you have brought us to a great fossil site."

On the drive back to the Park headquarters, five Geiger counters are ticking over fast.

We are desperately hoping that we have it all wrong about Akhram and that he doesn't get nasty. I watch his hands in the rear-view mirror and try to keep him talking.

That night, we double check the locks on our cabin door. At first light we are gone.

TWELVE
SURVIVAL AT SANDSPIT

KARACHI, 1985

"Eeeaaaagh!"

Maria's scream is long and loud.

Out in the moonlit dunes, weeping turtles continue their egg-laying ritual. The Locks wake. Flashlights shine. Voices are raised. Janna rushes to Maria's bedside.

"Maria, what is it? What's the matter with your feet?"

I join them. "Hey! Where's all that blood coming from?"

In between sobs, Maria gets her story out.

"I was dreaming, Mum. It was awful! I was down the beach, covered with sand, with just my head and toes showing. Something was nipping my feet. I looked and it was Dad pinching my toes. Then the nipping got harder, but I couldn't move and I couldn't speak. I tried to scream, but nothing came out. Then I woke up, and it wasn't Dad and it wasn't a dream. Something dark was chewing my toes!" Maria grabs a tissue and blows hard. "Then I remembered that yesterday a rat gnawed through a plastic peanut butter jar and Dad was blocking up holes in the kitchen."

She dissolves into her appalled mother's arms. "Mum, that rat was eating me!"

✻

It took us seven hours to drive from our home in Mithi in the desert to the beach hut near Karachi.

There are not many places where a foreign family can get away, particularly if they have teenage daughters. At Sandspit Beach we can relax on the sand, swim, read, watch the turtles, ride horses and camels, or just chill out.

Surge ... swiiiissh.

Surge ... swiiiissh.

The surf sends me to sleep.

Sindhi well diggers, starving people and desert scorpions are all far, far away.

Like chunky beads, scores of holiday houses adorn Sandspit's sandy white throat. Some are ostentatious, others, like ours, are very basic. On Fridays, families from Karachi come down and open their beach houses for the day. They seldom sleep in them. There is cricket on the shore, picnics on the sand, horses galloping and camels complaining.

Young males flaunt their manliness by wading into the sea in their *shalwar kamiz*. A few daring young women do likewise, emulating the song-and-dance sirens in the popular Bollywood movies. Every year, the surf sucks some of these adventurers into its watery maw. Few can swim, and most are fully clothed in *shalwar* suits. After all, to expose more than ankles and wrists would be indecent.

The longer I'm in Pakistan, the more I become like a Pakistani husband and father. I too resent men ogling my women, particularly when the young bloods take liberties that are blatantly counter-cultural. Perhaps it's the Western videos they watch. They get the idea that all Western females are loose.

At Sandspit we have the place entirely to ourselves, except on Fridays. Fridays are red alert days. On Fridays, countless young men try to ogle my women. The girls resentfully call them "Teds".

My primal instincts come to the fore. I become like an ever-watchful sheepdog guarding my flock. When he's not riding along the beach on a camel or a horse, Matthew helps with surveillance.

"Oh Sir, can you tell me the time?"

Oldest trick in the book.

"Sir, I am thirsty. Do you have a drink of water?"

Second oldest trick in the book.

"Sir, which country do you come from?"

Well up on the list.

"Sir, my English is to be too weak. Can I talk with you?"

Maybe another time and another place, when my daughters aren't ten feet away.

"Sir, can I take your photo?"

That will be a negative. You'll just try and get my females in the background, then brag to your friends afterwards.

Not surprisingly, by midday Friday we usually give up. We lock the hut and drive along the coast, pausing here and there to enjoy the cliffs and sand.

But today is Monday. The beach is empty. It's just us. Janna and the girls can throw off the enveloping *shalwar kamiz* and enjoy the sun in bathing suits. Matt successfully haggles for much cheaper horse and camel rides.

Hold on! In the distance I see a large vehicle approaching. It looks like a university bus bringing a group of male students for the day.

I know exactly what will happen.

In the West, that bus would go right past us. With all that unending sand, the visitors would be delighted. "Look, no people! Hooray! We're away from everything and everyone."

Not in Pakistan. People must be near people.

The bus crawls along the road behind the beach houses. Its passengers are feeling bereft and let down. I know what they will be saying.

"Look! There is no one here! Oh, no!"

But sure enough they find people. We are the only souls on the mile-long beach, and magnetically, the bus pulls in right beside our vehicle. They pile out and lay out their blankets directly in front of our beach-hut.

By this time, the sheepdog has worked the swim-suited females back into the shearing shed to put their wool back on. In full fleece, they reappear to read and take the breeze on the narrow veranda. I take up a commanding position to protect my pride.

By late afternoon we are on our own again. We spend the early evening playing Scrabble in the glow of the gas lamps.

At nine o'clock, Matt grabs a flashlight. "Come on, Dad! You said we'd check on the turtles tonight."

"OK, everyone," I announce, "let's go."

Out on the moonlit sand, the two-hundred kilogram turtles have scooped out great holes and seem oblivious to our presence. Tears stream down their faces as they deposit hundreds of eggs in the depressions.

"Why are they crying?" asks Maria.

"Perhaps they are weeping for their children," says Janna, "the ones that won't survive the seagulls and barracudas. And, of course, the turtle soup."

"I've read that they can swim up to fifteen hundred miles away," Angela chimes in, "then come back to the exact place where they hatched out."

"Wow!" says Matt. "How do they do that, Dad?"

"I don't know, son. I guess it's another one of creation's mysteries, waiting to be solved."

It has been a magical night, sharing the blazing stars with those amazing creatures. I'm glad the Government of Pakistan has set aside this area as a sanctuary.

※

Maria shrieks again. "A rat, Mum! I've been eaten by a rat!"

Janna barks out orders. "Grant! Find that thing and kill it! Angela! Get the Dettol from the first aid box! Matt! Put the kettle on the gas stove!"

I light the gas lamp and start moving everything that is at floor level. A shadow skims between some boxes and our suitcases. The cricket bat comes down hard. *Eat my daughter, would you? Take that! And that! And that!* The first blow was all that was needed, but I slam it several times. It's a big, but skinny, female. I note the tiny teats on her belly and feel a tinge of regret. Like me, she was doing her best to help her family survive.

Janna is swabbing Maria's toes. She arrows a glance my way.

"Grant, I've just about had it with this place. It's one thing to have rats chewing up food and clothes, but when they start on my kids, that's it! This is the third time we've been here now, and, yes, it's great to get away. But to what? It always takes at least a day to get the place clean, and then you never know what will happen next—like the first time we came down. I was absolutely terrified."

She wasn't the only one.

※

In the middle of the night there was a banging on the door. It got louder and louder.

"Let us in," the voices demanded. "You have to let us in."

No way. Not with my wife and girls here.

"*Arp koun hai?*" I called out. "Who are you?"

"We are Coast Guard. You have to let us in."

It wasn't a Friday. We were all alone at Sandspit. We were new to the country, with limited language and vulnerable. I was afraid they would knock that flimsy door down. I was supposed to be responsible for my family. The beam of my flashlight betrayed my shaking hand.

I bustled the terrified family into one of the bedrooms.

"Lock that door, Janna!" I hissed. "And don't unlock it till I've sorted this out!" I turned back to the shouts coming from outside the door.

"What is your name?" the voices demanded.

"My name is Lock. My family is here, my son, my wife and daughters. Come back tomorrow!"

Silence.

Maybe the cultural thing was sinking in. It's a disgrace to bust into a house where there are women.

"Just show us your face. Open the door!"

Like a farm windmill caught in a storm front, my mind was racing. *I've heard there's a lot of opium smuggling along this Makran coast. Perhaps these Coast Guards are just doing their duty. Or perhaps they're bored and want to lay eyes on this foreign family. Whatever, there's no way I'm opening that door.*

My brain scrambled another Urdu response. "*Manaasib nahi*—It is not fitting. *Cul waapis*—Come back tomorrow."

They held a noisy conference. I counted at least four voices. Then they left and never came back.

❋

Janna is bandaging Maria's toes. There is a tremble in her voice. "What if that rat had rabies?"

"Ok," I say, "first thing in the morning we're out of here and back to Karachi to find a doctor."

At the Aga Khan Hospital the doctor checks the toes, then looks up. "You are sure she has had the full course of rabies shots, Mrs Lock?"

Janna is looking paler than her daughter. She nods.

The doctor continues, "Otherwise, she will need a series of big injections, directly into her abdomen."

Janna fumbles in her handbag, pulls out Maria's medical booklet and thrusts the open page across the desk.

The doctor studies it and looks up. "Good! Did you wash and disinfect the bites?"

"Yes."

"Well, she should be OK. Come back if there is any change."

We didn't return to the hospital. And we never went back to Sandspit. The weeping turtles, the smugglers, the Teds and, no doubt, the rats all survived us.

THIRTEEN

WHO?

ADELAIDE, 2014

Open air. Blue dome. Sunshine. Shady trees. Writers. Communicators. Thinkers.

It's the annual Adelaide Writers' Week interviews. I take a seat in the shade and turn to the neatly dressed matron next to me. "Is this the 'Who Am I?' session?"

"Yes," she replies, pointing to a page in her program. Then she lowers her voice. "I think they're gay."

The guest authors are climbing the steps of the open-air stage. Good. I want to know what they think about this seminal question: "Who am I?"

I turn to Mrs Neatly. "Too bad I can only stay for half the session. Should be interesting."

The amplifiers come alive. "Welcome, ladies and gentlemen. Let me introduce our guests." In no time we know their names and writing achievements. In Pakistan, it would have taken twice as long with only half the information: garlands and lofty words must be lavished on such respected visitors. Our interviewer wants to give the speakers maximum time to deal with that question: "Who am I?"

Unfortunately, by the time I have to leave, they have only talked about family influences. I pull out my white cane and head up the path, wondering whether they will sink their notable teeth into this subject of all subjects. Will they link it entirely to sexuality: maleness, femaleness or in-between-ness? I don't understand in-between-ness, but I have a friend who struggles with it.

As the ratchet in my retina crushes the last fragments of my central vision, it's a challenge to keep cool and not get angry. Yes, I have a different set of struggles. I have my challenges, but sexual in-between-ness is something I haven't had to deal with. Unlike my friend Stephen.

He is in our writers' group and is a sharp wordsmith and an intuitive reader. That's why I often ask him to read out my contributions for me.

Stephen is slim, married and has a lovely wife and two grown-up kids. "Did you notice his hands?" Janna said on the way home from a patio meal in their home in the hills. I shake my head. "The slender fingernails, so nicely manicured?"

Well, I couldn't see those details. I was more interested in the in-depth discussion we were having about his visit to South-East Asia.

Things became clear after a couple of weeks. Stephen wrote a letter to the group.

> Hi, Writing Pals!
>
> This is Stephen here, or "Stephanie" as I call myself in female mode.
>
> For those of you who have been wondering about my earrings and long straggly hair, that's just my female side coming out. I have struggled with the issues since I was little, but only recently realised that it is more that I want to be female than just to dress female. The name for that, I have discovered only recently, is transgender. Apparently, we all fit on the transgender spectrum from uber-female to uber-male. Well, I am somewhere in the middle.
>
> The subject is not taboo, so feel free to chat and joke about it, or ask me about it.
>
> Cheers,
>
> Stephen

Stephen received a lot of supportive emails from the group. We still see him as a friend and writing colleague. I wrote back:

> Stephen, I've had to work through a few tunnels of uncertainty in my life, but not the kind you have at present. I actually think there is a lot more that defines who we are than our sexuality.
>
> All the best.
>
> Grant

✳

As my white stick leads me away from the discussion, I'm thinking about the people who raised me.

Dad. A hard-working, innovative farmer. Ambitious. Always wanted more land, regardless of what the overdraft looked like. Perhaps that's because his father died young in that horse-bolting accident and Dad had to quit school early and tough it out to hold onto the bit of land they had. I inherited a strong work ethic from Dad—perhaps too strong at times. He was witty and passionately loved his tennis. Hated to lose. Hated for me to lose.

Then there was Mum. What a woman! She, too, had it tough. Only a teenager when her mother died. Her father had already gone, so it was up to Muriel Chipp Hamp, the oldest of four, to shepherd the others along. She was the best cook in our district: crumbed lamb chops, Scotch fillets, German yeast cake, trifles, brandy snaps. Mmm-mmm! A natural organiser, she and her friends turned on a spread at the annual cattle sales we had on the property. You could hear the city-based clients and auctioneers walking to their plane, in between quiet burps: "Ahhh, these country cooks! They are something else!"

Yes, both my parents had grit, stickability and humour. They were people you enjoyed being around. Too bad other women put pressure on their long-term unity. Dad even ordered a nice new car for his smooth-talking city hairdresser. Perhaps she took more off than just his hair. No doubt the guilt was biting on the six-hour drive back home. Like a kid who had stolen too many cookies, he had to let it out. It was the family partnership account, not his own, so we zapped into our local bank manager's office and stopped the cheque. My gutsy mother stuck it out, but in the end there were no winners.

Theirs was not the whole influence on who I am, but upbringing definitely shaped me. Another "shaper" was the out-of-place guy who pulled his caravan up outside our country school yard.

The first day you meet you are friends.
The next day you meet you are brothers.
AFGHAN PROVERB

FOURTEEN

THE LAMBORGHINI AND THE BIG STICK

ADELAIDE, 2015

Has something like this ever happened to you?
    You look at your watch. The kids will be at the school gate in ten minutes. You might make it after all. But the "less than twelve items" line at the checkout has stalled. That's when you notice the guy up in front. He's unloading a whole trolley-load of shopping and they are actually putting it through. *Hey, that's not right! That's not fair!*
    You finally get to the school and—yes!—there is one parking space left. You have your indicator on and you're turning the wheel. There's a dark flash. A big black SUV cuts in front of you and pushes into your spot. You stomp on the brake and shout, "Hey, that's not fair!" She doesn't hear you. She springs out, gives a quick "I'm-in-a-bigger-hurry-than-you" wave and strides off. *It's just not right.*
    There is a Pakistani proverb: *"Jiski lahti, uskibhans*—He who has the big stick gets the buffalo." And every day, big sticks are taking buffaloes from little people, all over the world. It's just not right. It's just not fair.
    It seems there is an innate demand for justice among human beings. Sure, it varies in tone from place to place, and it can often be couched in terms of honour and revenge. But I reckon we are all wired for justice. Half the TV news is filled with this deep-seated desire to see justice. The child molester who murders his victim and is finally caught after twenty years. The purse-snatcher who bashes up the frail widow. The smooth financial manager who creams off the life-savings people have entrusted to him. The military dictator who rolls his tanks into a neighbouring country.
    That desire for justice must be satisfied. Some pusher-inners are brought to justice in this life, but not all of them. It's not fair that they

live out their lives, go to the grave and are never caught. It's not fair for the murdered, molested child or the parents. It's not fair for the victims of the big companies selling shonky, sometimes life-threatening products. Deep down, we demand that all the pusher-inners get what they deserve—if not in this life, then somehow in the next.

Stephen Hawking says that values like love and justice come from our own individual minds. That means that Mother Teresa and Stalin, Nelson Mandela and Pol Pot are all just following the morality built up in their own minds. But we say, "No way! That's not right!"

Where did this universal wiring for justice come from? If the survival of the fittest is all that counts for humanity, the "That's not fair!" protesters would have been exterminated by the chomping jaws of the "Too bad, that's irrelevant!" monsters. But it *is* relevant, because deep down everyone wants some kind of justice.

So what has all that got to do with the question "Who am I?" In an inverse sort of way, it helps find the answer. The haemoglobin of justice inexplicably pumping through our veins points to something beyond ourselves.

But the really pivotal question to be asked—and you won't have to go to Google for the answer—is this: "Did you create yourself?"

Please don't say, "No, I didn't; I just happened somehow." If a Lamborghini dropped out of the sky right in front of us, we wouldn't say, "It just happened somehow." We'd look up into the sky to locate the source.

And just as the Lamborghini demands a maker, I reckon the existence of you and me, and our desire for fairness and justice, demands a source, a maker, as well.

So if there is an intelligent designer out there, perhaps I ought to find out what he thinks about me. Hold on, though—maybe he wants to thump me, because one way or another I've done a bit of pushing in myself. Or he might want to make demands on me. I don't like the thought of that.

Maybe I'll just do the ostrich thing and say he isn't there. I'll be a sophisticated ostrich though. I'll put on a researcher's coat, use lots of big words and numbers, and stick my head into a microscope or telescope instead of in the sand. "There is no God," I'll say. "We don't need one."

Today, some of the strongest voices in the media are saying that sophisticated, civilised humankind has got past the ancient notion of a creator. We make a super-intellectual mask of ostrich leather that conveniently blindfolds us as we strut through our lives. "There is no intelligent designer behind it all," we say. "Science and its proven laws tell us so."

But does anyone ask, "Where did those laws come from? Why are they consistent? Why is there order among them instead of chaos?"

The high priests of the temple of modern meaning, great men like the David Attenboroughs and Stephen Hawkings, should be the first to be amazed at what they share with us. They should be the first to acknowledge that it all points to an intelligent designer. Respectfully, I suggest that their kind of blindness seems greater than my macular kind. I do not want to worship in their temple.

In that temple of no meaning, one simple question challenges the deepest roots of thought: "Why is there something instead of nothing?" I think Richard Rodgers and Oscar Hammerstein, in *The Sound of Music*, were thinking clearly when they wrote, "Nothing comes from nothing; nothing ever could."

The Attenboroughs and Hawkings continue to amaze us with revelations of what lies beyond us and within us. And I say, "Mindboggling! Keep going!" Because all of that just increases my desire to stand in awe and praise of that intelligent designer whom so many are afraid to meet. But we have no need to fear. The moral and meaning director of the cosmos, the personality that drives the universe, wants to satisfy our craving for justice, and he wants us to know his personality of love.

I can hear you saying, "Hold on, Grant! That philosophical stuff is all well and good, but if you were black, or an Afghan widow, or one of the millions of unemployed, or illiterate, or someone struggling with in-between-ness—or if you lost the rest of your limited vision—wouldn't that affect your view of who you are?"

Yes, all those things can say something about my status in life, my job, my family, my sexuality, my education, my location. But in the end it is much deeper than that.

Who am I? I am Grant Lock, a uniquely created being. I do not have all the answers, and I have my own struggles, particularly with my failed central vision. But I know that I am wanted, and I belong.

I enjoy the creator, who reveals himself, in part, through his amazing creation. That creation tells me he loves order and variety. The laughter of colour, light and shade, simple and complex. He loves to surprise us as we search and discover. It is as though he is screaming for our attention.

And that scream could not have been louder than his death-defying shout of love on the cross: "It is finished!" At that moment, he brought together our desire for meaning, our demand for justice and our passion to be loved.

Stephen, my friend at the writers' group, is now Steph or Stephanie. My heart aches for him as he works his way through in-between-ness. "But Grant," he says, "you say there's some kind of creator. If that is true, why did he do it?" He arcs his hands towards me, then back to himself. "Why did he make us?"

At that moment I am really glad that Janna picked out a kid's book for our grandsons. It came up with the answer, in profoundly simple words: "God has so much love he wanted to give some away."

There are still questions, but for me, he answers the big ones.

FIFTEEN

ROAD THERAPY

KARACHI, 1986

Karachi city has a population rivalling that of the whole of Australia. I soon learnt the local style of driving. It's the same as anywhere else in Pakistan, except noisier. More vehicles. More horns. Fewer spaces to fight for.

The horn on the Toyota Hilux may have been fine while driving through the ordered cities of Japan, but it is a rather weak bleat amid the roaring cacophony of Karachi's on-road circus. It's like being in a crowded room—everyone talks louder and louder to be heard. So I headed off to the vehicle accessories bazaar, fitted extra horns and rejoined the fray.

In Australia, if there is one small toot, every driver stiffens with indignation. Grips tighten. Knuckles whiten. Heads rotate and rearview mirrors are scanned.

"Who's tooting?"
"Is someone tooting at *me?*"
"I haven't done anything wrong!"
"Some people are *so* impatient!"

Is it any wonder there are so many stressed-out drivers in Australian cities? All the way from the toot to the destination, their minds are continually replaying the offensiveness of it all.

Back in Pakistan, drivers have less need for counsellors and psychologists. That's because they get rid of their repressed emotion by expressing it on their horns. It's mile after mile of healthy therapy.

There is the "I'm coming through!" blast.
The "move over!" blast.
The "what do you think you're doing?" blast.
The "Hey! That was my space!" blast.
The celebratory "Hah, I've finally got past you!" blast.

The occasional "Thank you" double toot.
The "We're having a wedding" drawn-out honk.
And, of course, the "Pakistan just won the cricket" sonic celebration.
Then there is Pakistan's on-road repentance therapy. If you want to say sorry after cutting in or somehow offending another road user, it's easy. You just raise your hand and grip an ear lobe. Every driver knows that means, *"Tobah, tobah—*I repent, I'm sorry."

But in Australia, what do we do? I can be genuinely repentant, but if I wave a hand or fingers in any kind of fashion, people will probably think I'm saying "Get lost!" or "Too bad, that's life!" or something worse. So we drive on with our unresolved, mixed-up emotions. We return home to bark at the husband, or the wife, or the kids, or the dog.

SIXTEEN

HOLDING ON

THAR DESERT, 1987

Janna. "Oh no! It's starting again." Racing heart. Fear. Breathing speeds up. More fear. Hands shaking. Body on fire inside. Feeling faint. Chest pains. "Am I going to die?" Slip a pill—doesn't seem to work. "Grant, why aren't you back? You get back so late when you drive into Hyderabad. The *dacoits,* bandits—they're breeding up. They operate at night. Better if you had company. But Keemo is off at his nephew's wedding. Always weddings. Always funerals. I could have gone. But my classes—the local girls are overlooked too often."

Grant. "If only the Thar Desert Aid meeting had finished earlier. Budgets. Updates. Bishop raised the planned women's clinic. Pakistani staff nearly ready to go. Two more pot plants for our sandy yard. More *sufeda* seedlings—those Aussie red gums do well in the desert. The hardware store. The grocery bazaar. The vegetable bazaar. Decent potatoes, not black marbles."

Janna. "Chest pain getting worse. Can't think. Giddy. Hearing dim. Yes, it's stress, anxiety. But there must be an answer. Blacky, the dog, sleeping outside the door. But what can she do? Ten o'clock. Locals well in bed. Just the Hindu singers at the graveyard. Gotta lie down. More chest pain. Am I going to die? Gotta leave a note. Wish there were some other foreigners in this town. Where are you, Grant? Where are you, God?"

Grant. "They sure are generous when they call this sand track a road. What's that up ahead? A small camel? No, a big donkey, standing across the track. Flash my lights. Doesn't move. *Toot toot!* 'Out of the way, stupid donkey, I'm already late!' Deaf as well as dumb. Can't drive around—dunes on each side. Give him a soft nudge with the bull bar. Still won't move. The grandfather of stubbornness. Give him a solid thump. Can't believe it—he just fell over, like a cut-out wooden prop from a nativity play. I swear he's grinning. Still no way around. Jump out and give Grandpa Stubborn some unkind Aussie outback names and a hefty kick. Still no movement. Groan. Flick the front-wheel hubs to engage the four-wheel drive. Reverse 150 metres to a dip in the dune. Bush-bash half a kilometre around the dunes. Re-join the track. Only five more minutes to Mithi."

※

Janna is fast asleep. She looks pale, but her breathing is steady. There is a note beside her bed.

"Grant. It's 10.15. I think I'm dying. Here's a list of the medication I've taken, for what it's worth. I love you always. Janna."

She's had another attack. Back then we didn't know what to call it. I should have been here. I planned to be back by dark, but as usual there were too many things on the agenda. Even now when I am here, I feel so useless—I pray and bring sweet tea, while she sits up on the bed, holding her chest. But it's not a heart attack. Her heart is fine.

※

Two years later we are on home assignment back in Adelaide. Janna has persevered through various levels of anxiety, depression and panic attacks, with only limited enlightenment from the medicos. We are looking for answers.

Bronwyn Fox is addressing a group of us. We have all seen a small ad in the local paper.

"If you have some of these symptoms, come and join us." I read the symptoms out. Janna's eyes widen. "Are we finally going to get to the bottom of this, Grant?"

"It's called a panic attack," Bronwyn says. "Until recently, most doctors have been blind to how it works. It can mimic all sorts of pain and other symptoms, even a heart attack. Fear fills your body. You think you're going to die."

I can see people nodding all around the room.

"I know," Bronwyn says quietly. "I've been through it all many times. So many times." She looks around the room at people from all walks of life. Fancy jackets. Tatty coats. All hanging on her words.

"But there is a way out," she says. "I'll help you understand it and get on top of it. I'll teach you cognitive therapy. You'll take charge of it with your mind and think your way through the fear." She pauses. "But the first thing you need is this."

With that she pulls out an empty brown paper bag. She has our undivided attention.

"When the attack starts, the fear starts and you usually breathe too fast. It's called hyper-ventilation. You lose the right balance of carbon dioxide. You grow faint, get more fearful, breathe faster. It's all a vicious cycle."

I am getting excited. She seems to know what she is talking about. The medicos haven't shed any light on this, but now it has a name. I feel certain we are about to have a revelation.

"But what has the paper bag got to do with it?" I blurt out.

"Simple," she says. "You just hold it over your mouth and breathe slowly. It corrects the carbon dioxide balance."

Jaws are dropping all around. "And if you don't have a bag, just hold your breath, then breathe slowly."

Janna and I look at each other. If only we had known. It was the start of a journey.

Thank you, Lord, for Bronwyn Fox. This woman has 'been there, done that' and shared the breakthrough with so many.

We can now return for another term in Pakistan.

❋

RECOMMENDED READING

Bronwyn Fox's invaluable book, *Power over Panic*, is published by Penguin Books. Her website is www.panicattacks.com.au.

Also *Living with it: A Survivor's Guide to Panic Attacks* by Bev Aisbett (HarperCollins).

Patience is bitter
but its fruit is sweet.
AFGHAN PROVERB

SEVENTEEN

LOST

ADELAIDE, 2014

Janna wakes up shaking.

It's six years since we returned from our twenty-four years in Pakistan and Afghanistan, but she still gets flashbacks. Black tea with sugar helps, and so does a debriefing. I'm not very good at that, but I am learning. I squeeze her shoulders and listen.

"I know it's a flashback, Grant," she says in a panting whisper. "But it's so real. So many of the places are places I've been. So many of the things are things that have happened to me. But it's all mixed up."

"Go on," I say.

"I was lost. It was getting dark and I couldn't find my way home. The streets were familiar, yet unfamiliar. That's if you could call them streets. Just twisty lanes. Some mucky, some stony. Some sandy, like back in the desert. Bare concrete flats, and crumbling mud-brick houses behind crumbling mud-brick walls. The walls seemed to be saying, 'We're doing our best. But how can we stand here in the midst of the fighting and neglect? No one comes to repair our cracks. No one comes to re-render us with a layer of fresh clay-mud. No one cares.'

"Bonny was with me. At the end of a blind alley we stared at another of those walls. Plastic bags and leaves, like us, were looking for a way out. We turned back. 'Have to keep going, Bonny,' I said.

"We were dressed like locals, but at that time of the evening all self-respecting women are behind their walls squatting beside their kerosene burners and preparing the daal. I could feel the men staring at us. I pulled my head-covering lower over my brow and tried to ignore them. Boys hurried past with sideways glances. They carried armfuls of fresh-smelling naan bread, hot from the tandoor shop.

"Then I recognised a familiar pile of garbage on a familiar corner. I tugged on Bonny's sleeve. 'This way!' I said. Yes, I had been lost, but until then I hadn't really been afraid in those ever-changing lanes. You know how I've learnt to feel secure when there are many people around. It's when I'm alone in an empty street that my pulse starts racing. Like back in Kabul. Do you remember when that boy followed me for a whole empty block with his arm raised, pointing a gun at me? He was only a few steps behind me. Even then I was more angry than scared. I just kept walking. 'How dare you,' I thought. 'You arrogant pup!' And when I turned the corner into a busy street, he decided not to follow. But if he had flashed a knife, I don't know what I would have done, particularly when the street was so empty. Long ago I told you, Grant, that I could accept being shot, but to have my throat cut, that filled me with fear."

I am nodding slowly, then as an after-thought she adds, "But the street wasn't completely empty. There was one man …" Her voice drifts a bit. "He was dressed like one of the Taliban … big black turban, beard, waistcoat. He just appeared on the footpath. No doors or gates. Just those high walls."

I am trying to recall the details. "What was he doing?"

"He just stood there. Arms folded, passive look. I didn't know if he was supporting the kid, or … protecting me. As I was about to turn the corner I looked back. The kid had stopped, but the man was still there, arms folded. Then … he just disappeared."

"Went back into his house I suppose,"

"No Grant, I told you. There were no gates or doors or parked vehicles anywhere near where he was standing." Her voice is quieter than ever. "He was an Angel."

We are silent for a while then she takes up her story again.

"We hurried past more familiar, buzzing rubbish piles. As we turned the last corner, everything seemed to change. Our house was shabbier than ever, and outside our door there were poles. And tied to those poles were men. And around the poles were bearded men with guns. They were chanting *'Allah O Akbar!'* and shooting into the air. I could see the eyes of the men on the poles. They knew they were about to die.

"The beards with guns hadn't seen us. 'We must go back, Bonny,' I whispered. And then we were lost again. Lost in the sandy streets of Mithi in the desert, then the dusty back alleys of Peshawar, then the muddy lanes of Kart-e Sey in Kabul. Lost. Lost location. Lost direction. Lost identity."

"So what did you do?"

"Several houses ahead of us a door moved. It was a woman watching. She beckoned me urgently with that downward wave of Central Asia. She wanted to help. I spoke to her in Dari, but she couldn't understand. Bonny spoke to her in Pashtu, and still she didn't understand. She was from another language group altogether.

"We moved on and it was getting darker. It's not wise to be out in the dark. That's when we heard the singing. 'Listen,' Bonny said. She pointed towards a window where there was once glass. 'It's coming from over there.' Like moths towards a flame, we moved towards that singing. We recognised the tune. It wasn't loud, but it was welcome thunder in our ears.

"A man at the door let us in. 'We must find Mr Anderson's house,' Bonny said. 'You know, the tall foreign man with red hair. And his wife is tall, too. Do you know where they live?' He wanted to help, but he couldn't understand us. Yet I could understand him. When he spoke, he kept saying, 'We have no pastor. We have no pastor. We just meet here to sing.' Then a boy ran from the gloom waving his arms. In a few moments they were all gone, in their drab garb, lost in the crowd. Again we were lost in the dark."

Janna starts to sob again. "You know what it's like, Grant. There were no street lights or numbers on houses or names on streets. Just those walls. High, mud-brick walls."

She reaches for a tissue.

"Who is Bonny?" I ask.

"One of those lovely girls from England. Well, she was *like* them, even though we never knew a Bonny. She met me in the bazaar and asked me to take her to the Andersons. I said I would because they were near us." Janna looks at me. "I know, I know, the Andersons weren't in Kabul, but we did stay with them in Adelaide. It's all mixed up." She takes a breath and exhales. "But it does help to talk about it."

I pull her closer. "And how did it end?"

"Like all the others. Half of me says: I want to be there because that is where I belong. And the other half of me is afraid of the lostness, and the knives. So often I am running. Running, running."

Yes, it's another of Janna's debilitating flashbacks, a symptom of post-traumatic stress. Not surprising after all she has been through. The good thing is that these days it's easier to talk.

EIGHTEEN

FLOWERS AND PHONES

ADELAIDE, 2014

"What's going to happen in Afghanistan now that most of the foreign troops are out?"

I've just finished speaking at a current affairs group, and it's time for questions.

I survey the gathering. "Good question! To help answer that, let me ask you all a few other questions. First, why were our troops in Afghanistan?"

There is a quick response from halfway back. "Because the Americans said so."

"Mmm, that's partly true. We do have treaty partners to consider. But what was the *primary* reason the Americans went into Afghanistan?"

A shout comes from the back. "Oil!"

I shake my head. "No. But that would have been a factor in the Iraq war a few years later."

As I wait for the next answer, my mind is ticking over. *This is all recent history, and it's the longest war Australia has ever been involved in. This current affairs group must have some sharper heads out there.*

I am not disappointed. A small grey-haired woman pipes up from the front. "To stop al-Qaeda."

"Absolutely correct. And what was the trigger for that?"

"9/11," she fires back.

"That's right. Bin Laden was in Afghanistan training anti-Western terrorists to fly planes into American skyscrapers, bomb Australians in Bali nightclubs and attack trains in the British underground."

"And what about the Taliban?" someone calls out.

"OK," I say, "let's get things into perspective. Here's the next question. Has anyone been to Afghanistan?"

Most heads shake vigorously, but one female hand goes up.

"When did you go, ma'am?"

"When I was twenty. I travelled across Asia in 1975. Kabul was a lovely city. Big mountains all around."

"Right," I say. "They were the good years. A lot of tourists and adventurers travelled through Afghanistan in the '70s."

"So what happened?" asks a male voice.

"I'll give you a thirty-second overview. The local communist party ousted the king. Then on Christmas Day 1979 the Soviet Union rolled in. After ten years of fighting, they were pushed out. Then the victorious mujahidin freedom fighter groups fought among themselves. Finally, the Taliban rose to the top and were running things up till December 2001."

"Along with all their hard-line sharia law," pipes up my front-row enthusiast. "And made life extra tough for women."

"That's right. No education for females. Women charged with adultery were stoned or shot. Men had to wear beards, like the Prophet Muhammad. Women had to be completely covered and stay home. No music, no television, etc. And the Taliban said to the Americans and the rest of the world, 'If you want to stop al-Qaeda, you'll have to fight us, too. They are fellow Muslims, they are guests in our country—and furthermore, our boss's daughter is one of Osama bin Laden's wives.'

"So the Taliban were pushed back into the mountains and over the border into Pakistan, or they just disappeared back into their villages."

A hand goes up a few rows back. "But aren't they regaining ground?"

"Correct. Particularly in the south and east. And they earn a lot of money from the floral industry."

"Floral industry?" says the mystified voice of someone having trouble melding images of tough turbaned fighters and flower shops.

I try to hide my smirk. "They get a healthy cut from the red poppy fields." There are a few grunts of recognition, and I hear the word "heroin" from different parts of the hall. "Yes, heroin production is growing, and Afghanistan already produces over ninety percent of the world's supply. A lot of black-market money corrupts the society from top to bottom. And, in Taliban areas, if you want to grow something else, you could be looking down the barrel of a gun."

"So what's the chance of peace?" asks the original questioner.

"There's an outside possibility of a political settlement with the government. But the Taliban will push for the last of the foreign troops to leave, and women's rights, tenuous as they are, will be traded downwards. In the meantime, the Taliban will gain as much ground as they can with their roadside bombs, suicide vests, ambushes and kidnappings. It's now up to the retrained Afghan army and police force to take up the fight against them on their own."

The questioner waves his hand again. "In your book you said that Pakistan's army was secretly supporting the Taliban in Afghanistan."

"That's true. We knew it back then. These days, it's common knowledge. Pakistan was afraid that its arch-rival, India, would gain too much influence in Afghanistan, so they quietly supported the Afghan Taliban as a hedge against that. But, as I said in the book, Pakistan would ultimately be stung by the tail of the scorpion it was feeding, and that is now happening. Pakistan is fighting the Taliban within its own borders, and they are reviewing their position."

I motion for further questions. A man stands at the back. "Has all the international money poured into Afghanistan done any good?"

"Yes," I reply. "Schools, hospitals, clinics, roads, women's rights and more. But huge amounts have slipped off the back of the truck." I grimace. "Sometimes the truck itself disappears. Just remember, this is the third most corrupt country in the world."

There are a few groans as I go on.

"But one of the big success stories is in mobile phones. Two-thirds of the country has some kind of access to a mobile phone, even if they have to climb the side of a mountain to get coverage. That kind of communication is vital. And there are a lot of TV and radio stations now."

My grey-haired source of wisdom at the front raises a hand. "If, after thirty-five years of fighting, they are able to come to a settlement with the Taliban, what is the economic future for the country?"

"I know there are a lot of very big 'ifs', but the country could have a good future."

"Really?" says a doubting voice from my left.

"Well, it's estimated they have a trillion dollars' worth of minerals waiting to be mined. Copper. Iron. And lithium—the scarce stuff that goes into mobile phone batteries. Plus some oil and gas. They are plonk in the middle of potentially huge trade routes. International companies want to pump gas from central Asia across Afghanistan to hungry markets in Pakistan, India and China. There is even talk of major railroads linking China with Europe. It could be the Silk Road all over again, but without the camels."

"Any chance?" an unconvinced voice calls out.

"There's always a chance," I say. "That's what the ordinary Afghan lives and struggles for. So much depends on leadership.

"They need a strong lead against corruption. But that's not easy. Leaders have to return the favours of the warlords and the ethnic groups that supported them in the elections. There is suspicion between ethnic groups. Animosity between the Sunni Muslims and the minority Shias. And an al-Qaeda remnant remains. The Taliban are slow to stop their terrorism and talk peace. And now Islamic State is getting into the act." I raise a finger. "I suspect that a lot of disaffected Taliban groups will swing over to join ISIS." I lower my hand. "Although a lot of girls now go to school, education is still a weak link, and the role of women in a developing society is almost ignored. Then there is all the black money from the opium business.

"But as the old Afghan proverb says: 'There is a path to the top of even the highest mountain.' That's why people continue to work and serve there. But it's a mighty high mountain."

In my peripheral vision I detect the moderator of the meeting fidgeting in her chair.

"One last question."

"Grant, do you think that you made any difference?"

I scan the room. "If your sight was restored, or if you received business training, or if micro-hydroelectricity was made available in your village, then, yes, you'd think that we made a difference. There is another Afghan proverb: 'Drop by drop, the river is made.'"

NINETEEN

THE PLAINCLOTHES POLICEMAN OF KABUL

KABUL, 2006

Strides to his car
like a movie star,
suited, booted.

Checks his revolver in full stride.
Am I secure
or should I hide?

Now the rich—
the rich like the police.
They get them off the hook.
"A little contribution, Sir, and we won't look."
But the poor—
the poor hate the custodians of the law.
"Give us money or you'll get more days in the cell,
with a shock or two."

But if you don't have the money,
what can you do?
While the rich sit at home with a DVD,
the poor beg for mercy and long to be free.

Wars and rumours of wars.
Broken lives, broken laws.
Broken women, broken men.
This is Afghanistan.

This is man.

Broken women, broken men,
Who can put them together again?
"Not I," said the sparrow, with his bow and arrow.
"Not I," said the little red hen.

But hey!
It takes more than a bird in a children's verse
to overcome hatred and the curse
of revenge, greed and the poppy,
with its roots in Helmund, and its powdery flowers
in the streets of the West.
White powder, white death.

Dollars from the lostness of Western consumers
buy guns and power for the lords of the land.
Drug-lords, War-lords, Lie-lords, Taliban,
all squeezing life from the common man.

Cancerous corruption,
fractured community,
women's rights in reduction,
illusory unity.

In East and West,
broken women and broken men.
Who can put them together again?
Not all the king's horses, not all the king's men.

But listen!

"I am the way," the holy man said.
"Revenge for your honour
is the way of the dead.

"Love your enemy.
Just let it go.
Forgive, and live.

"Serve your neighbour like a brother,
whether from your clan, or from another.

"Yes, let it go!" the Guru proclaimed,
"or your family will suffer
and your spirit stay lame,
and your country won't grow."

Suffocated by the lack of trust,
suffocated by Afghanistan's ancient dust.

A tilted load
won't reach its destination.
AFGHAN PROVERB

TWENTY

MOBILE MO

He doesn't like his name, so he has chosen one for himself. He is always in the latest vehicle with the most impressive horsepower. His friends call him Mr Mobile, so he's shortened it. He'll shake your hand with a firm, confident grip and say, "Just call me Mo!"

But now Mo is a wanted man. The posters are up all over town. "Dead or alive: Mobile Mo, the murderer."

That's why he is out in the backside of the desert.

He was once the coolest dude in town. Best university education. Everyone looked when Mo drove by. His household had class—well-heeled too. Nothing was too good for Mo. The smartest suits. The latest gadgets. He could mix it with the best.

Then everything changed.

The Boss was always building, and building big. He used the best architects and engineers around. Had a bit of trouble with the unions, but nothing new. They always want more pay, better conditions.

Now it so happens that one day Mo drove up, and the first thing he saw was one of the boss's henchmen beating up a workman. "Gotta stop this!" he said. "That guy is related to me!"

Before long the henchman was dead and there was blood on Mo's suit. He thought no one had seen it. But word soon got back to the Boss. Mo might have had friends in high places, but justice had to be done. That's when the posters went up and Mo decided to leave town, late at night.

Over the border, things are not so bad. The big rancher is a good guy, and he gives Mo a job. He suspects Mo is on the run: why else would a cultured man with soft hands and smart clothes turn up out there? But he doesn't ask questions. After all, his oldest daughter is pretty soft on the new arrival. "Daddy," slim Zippy says, "I met a nice man from over the border. Look at his suit. And he's strong, too—saved me from those toughs who always give us girls trouble when we line up for a drink."

No surprise that Mo and Zippy soon get hitched. After all, he won't be going back, and he needs a woman. Soon they have a couple of kids to boot.

Then comes the message. "Get back there, Mo! There's a new Boss—even worse than the last. The union has been dissolved. Those workers are getting it tough. You need to help."

"What can *I* do?" Mo protests. "I'm still wanted. There's no way I'm going back!" You can't blame him for complaining. He's mighty short of friends back there. But in the end, he goes.

When he turns up and says, "I've been sent to help," they say, "Yeah, yeah, Mo. Just like you did last time!" Then, at the construction site, after the Boss has finished laughing, he says, "Oĸ, Mo. You say you've been sent with this crazy message: 'Let my people go!' Well, in case you haven't noticed, they happen to be *my* people! And to be correct, they're not people! They're things! Slave things! And *my* things aren't going anywhere! So before I feed you to the crocodiles in the Nile, you've got two minutes to enlighten me. What is the name of the crazy who sent you?"

Moses straightens up and looks the Boss in the eye. "The name of the one who sent me is 'I Aм.'"

"What kind of name is that?" shouts Pharaoh.

"You're about to find out!" says Moses.

TWENTY-ONE

THE COMMANDER AND THE FLOOD

PESHAWAR, 1990

He looked impressive in his naval officer's uniform. I was in Grade 3 and hadn't seen anything like it. He drew his shining sword out of its scabbard and saw my bulging eyes.

"It's only a ceremonial sword," he said. I didn't even know what the word "ceremonial" meant. "Commander Harvey is my name." He stood to attention and saluted us. "At your service!" Then he reached for his piano accordion and started to sing.

I later found out that this retired British naval officer travelled the countryside waving his sword and telling stories. Great stories, about someone called Jesus. I'd heard a bit about this Jesus at Sunday school, but nothing like the way this strutting, sword-wielding Brit told those stories.

Somehow, I answered a question correctly. The Commander's clear eyes homed in on me. "Well done, lad! Here is your prize." I flicked open the little book and started picking out the words from the mass of small print. It was nothing like the language in our primary school library.

It started with a never-ending list of names, punctuated by another new word for me. Begat, begat, begat. It was hard going, and I wondered when the real story would start.

✹

Over the "sloosh, sloosh" sound of our mud-sweeping, there is a loud banging on our Peshawar gate.

Janna straightens up and rests on her broom. "The door bell's stopped working, Grant," she puffs. "You'd better see who it is."

In Pakistan, the power often goes out. This time it's the big rain and the local flood. Usually it's load shedding when there's not enough power to go around. Your lights go off unexpectedly and the fans slowly stop. Each spring, the Pakistani politicians make their annual promise: "Dear friends, this summer there will be no load-shedding!" Everyone knows that this will be true in the law-makers' mansions, but not for anyone else.

I slosh across our high-walled courtyard and swing open the gate. Our visitor is dressed like a Pakistani, but his speech is different. He extends a hand.

"I am Asadullah, your neighbour. Can I help?"

"What about your own house?"

A grin lights up his face. "Not a problem for us. We live on the second storey. I will bring brooms, and my brother."

It turns out he has three brothers as well as two sisters.

"How do you all fit in?" I ask as we push the stinking residue of the flood into the street.

"We manage. We have to manage. We are refugees from Afghanistan. It is our *kismet*, good fortune, that some of us have good jobs in aid organisations."

Yes, with employment, Asadullah and his family were among the lucky ones. Millions of jobless Afghans are roughing it in out-of-town refugee camps, having poured across the border to escape the Russian invaders. Of course, the Russians said they were invited by the leaders of the Afghan Communist Party, but the bulk of Afghans were dead against having the unbelieving infidels in their country.

The Soviets didn't just drop in to give a bit of kindly help. They had been preparing for this for decades. Preparing to take another step southward, with an eye toward the warm-water port of Karachi in neighbouring Pakistan. That's why they magnanimously built the huge highway through what was then the highest mountain tunnel in the world. When you drive up the Salang Highway and through the Salang Tunnel, you realise what an engineering achievement it was. It was all done in the name of foreign aid, but it sure made it easy to roll those tanks and trucks and soldiers southward.

In the name of foreign aid, they also built huge wheat silos and a large central bakery in Kabul. "What do we need those for?" the locals questioned. "We have our naan ovens at the end of every second street." But when those hungry Soviet troops arrived, guess where their bread was made? Not in the local tandoors.

Through Asadullah's mud-slushing assistance, we became good friends with our Afghan refugee neighbours. We found they were highly educated, including the use of some English. We shared meals and shared visits.

One day Asadullah's sister drew Janna aside. Sonia was a lovely young woman, modest and family orientated. She should have been married. But it's hard to find a husband for a sister who has a dark purple birthmark down the side of her face.

"Janna Jaan," she whispered. "I have something for you." She unclasped a thin chain from her neck, withdrew a hidden object and extended her hand. "This is for you, Sister Janna. You are a real Christian and I am not."

As Janna took the small engraved metal cross, she drew in her breath. "But Sonia, where on earth did you get it?" The Afghan scanned the room and did not answer. "Sonia, I can't take this. It's yours."

Janna is mystified. *Muslims don't wear crosses. The cross is the sign of the infidel unbelievers. They say Jesus was only a prophet. It's blasphemy to attribute more than that to him. He is definitely not God. They say he never died on that cross. Allah took him to heaven and one day will send him back to tell all the Christians that Islam is the only way. Did Sonia come across some suppressed Orthodox Christians when the Russians were educating her in Moscow?*

Sonia is speaking again. "Please take it, Janna Jaan. You are a real Christian. It belongs to you."

"Thank you, dear Sonia. I will pray for you."

The young woman's face brightens. "I would like that."

Next day Janna makes an announcement. "Grant, I am going to give a gift to Sonia." She waves a small book at me.

"I'm not so sure, Janna. What will her older brothers say?"

"I plan to ask them. It's the cultural and proper thing to do. I'm on my way now."

I rise. "I'll come with you."

Where the heart goes,
there follows the foot.
AFGHAN PROVERB

TWENTY-TWO

LIARS, TWISTERS AND FOOLS

PESHAWAR, 1990

We are in our neighbours' home, seated on *toshaks* on the floor and sipping green tea.

"I have this gift for Sonia," Janna says. "Asadullah, you are her oldest brother. I want to get your approval first."

Asadullah takes the small book. "It is truly kind of you to give a gift to Sonia, Janna Jaan." He carries on as though Janna was the first one to ever think of gift-giving when they do it all the time. They can be so gracious.

He carefully turns the pages and a look of interested awe drifts across his face. "You know, Janna Jaan, the Injil of Isa Masih is supposed to be recommended reading for Muslims. The Mullahs say it is corrupted, but many of us have lost confidence in those Mullahs and the way they put down women."

"Were the communists any different?" Janna asks.

"Oh, yes! At least for those of us in Kabul. They believed in education." He glances at his sister, who is pouring more tea. Sonia has a degree in architecture. "After the mujahidin pushed the Russians out, they started fighting among themselves." He gives a wry smile. "They all shouted 'Allah O Akbar!' as they rocketed each other. We were caught in the middle."

He stares out of the window for a moment, then turns his attention back to the book and begins to read out loud. It's the Gospel of Matthew the tax collector—the same gospel that Commander Harvey gave me outside the school gate.

"Chapter one. 'The book of the generation of Jesus Christ, the son of David, the son of Abraham. Abraham begat Isaac and Isaac begat Jacob.'"

Oh no! Not the begats. There's half a chapter of begats. I am wanting him to flick forward and get into the real story. I remember how I almost gave up in the middle of the genealogy.

But Asadullah ploughs on, his voice is getting more animated. "'And Jacob begat Judas, and Judas begat Perez.'" He looks up briefly. "This is so interesting, Mr Grant." He reads on, and his eyes digest another forty generations. Finally, he comes to the end: "'And Jacob begat Joseph, the husband of Mary, of whom was born Jesus, who was called Christ.'"

He pauses, looks up and reads the surprise on my face. "It is important to know the family connections, Mr Grant. It helps us know who we are. I have friends who can recite their line all the way back to the holy Prophet (peace be upon him)." He turns to Janna. "Yes, Sister Janna, you have my permission to give this to Sonia."

※

At home, I took a fresh look at that list, and it spoke to me. In this Jewish genealogy of the Promised One, there are some unlikely misfits. There are three reasons why Rahab shouldn't have rated a mention: she was a foreigner, a woman and a prostitute. Yet she is included. So is Ruth: another woman, another foreigner. The list includes murderers, liars, twisters and fools. They were accepted, and that means there is room for everyone—and room for me.

TWENTY-THREE

YOUNG LAWRENCE OF ARABIA

ADELAIDE, 2014

He could have stepped off the sand dunes of Saudi Arabia—flowing robe, red and white checked head-gear and sandals. I think he had a small beard: I can't focus these days. He spoke like an Aussie, and going by the bulge in the caftan, maybe he had consumed a kebab too many.

Yes, I am at the open day of the local mosque. Janna and I were welcomed by handsome young men and slim head-covered young women.

I know many Aussies are rattled by the head covering. They think Muslims are trying to push their Islamic ideas. And sometimes that might be true. But the head covering is not a problem for me. Hey, the Queen wears a head scarf when she goes walking at Balmoral in Scotland! And Janna always wore a head covering during our time in Islamic countries. But there is a huge difference between head covering and face covering. If the female greeters at our local mosque had had their faces covered, I would have been upset. To me it's un-Australian, it's not good for communication, and it's not good for security. End of story.

Janna and I split up and I find myself in a grassed area behind the mosque hall. Plenty of people and kids, a bouncy castle and face painting. I am enjoying the hospitality of the sausage sizzle when young Lawrence of Arabia approaches.

I give him the greeting of peace: "As salaam alekoom—Peace be with you." He returns the greeting: "Vaalekoom salaam—And peace also be with you." We start to chat.

His costume doesn't worry me too much. I have lived among a lot of Eastern outfits and regularly worn the baggy *shalwar kamiz*, which has to be one of the most comfortable garments in the world. But something about the way he presents himself makes me wary. He is in his mid-twenties, and among all the trousers and shirts he sticks out like the proverbial sore thumb. No doubt his outfit is meant to make a declaration of his commitment to Islam.

We introduce ourselves and I learn his name is Abbad. I ask him where he is from.

"Here in Adelaide," he says. "I converted to Islam about eighteen months ago. I looked at different religions, and halfway through studying Islam I could see it really had something."

I wipe some sauce from my face. He continues, "Starting the day with prayer is a great way to go. Sets the tone for the day."

I toss the tissue into a bin. "You're absolutely right. My wife and I have been doing that for years. Every morning we sit up in bed with a cup of tea and talk to God." I'm wondering if this new convert really approves of that kind of posture—Islamic prayers are done on the knees with the forehead bowed to the ground.

Abbad shares more about his appreciation of Islam. Then his tone changes. He starts swaying gently from side to side. "You know how seventy percent of Australians are below the poverty line …"

I don't have a chance to respond, but my brain has kicked into gear.

Hang on, Abbad—seventy percent? The last figure I heard was less than fifteen percent. And what's with the slow swaying? Are you just getting excited, or do you have some connection with the mystical Sufis?

He is still talking. "Well, it's funny how the bad people rise to the top."

Where are you going with this, Abbad? Sure, some bad people float to the top wherever you are, but in Australia we have mechanisms to scrape a fair bit of the flotsam off the surface. If you want to sing the praises of Islamic influence, better not crow too much. Eight of the ten most corrupt countries in the world are Muslim-majority nations.

He continues his slight swaying from one foot to the other. "And if they don't change, then they should be disposed of."

My eyes widen. This time, my tongue out paces my brain. "Disposed of? What do you mean?"

"They should be killed!"

I can't believe what I'm hearing. "Hold on, Abbad! Isn't that exactly what Islamic State advocates? If people don't fall into your way of thinking, then you can kill them. Even behead them."

He does a double take, knowing he can never take back the words that have escaped his lips. His swaying stops. He straightens. "No, no! I'm not for Islamic State. I'm not like them." He pauses. "You can't judge a religion by its works."

We chat for a few more stilted moments, then, in his Arabic kaftan and sandals, he excuses himself and shuffles off.

My jaw is still at half-mast. Did I hear him correctly? Yes, I did. And I am wondering who he has been listening to. Today this mosque is trying to say to Australia, "We're not like those terrorists"—and, lo and behold, I run into young Lawrence of Arabia. But perhaps he doesn't belong to this mosque. Perhaps, like me, he is just a visitor.

As I line up for a cup of tea, my mind is still churning. What was the meaning of that last statement, "You can't judge a religion by its works"? That's the second time I have heard it today. The first time was when I talked to Hussein, the cheerful greeter at the front door of the mosque. I didn't beat around the bush. I asked him the question all Australians silently want to ask, because we want the moderates to assure us they are against Islamic terrorism. "Hussein, when you see those heads being cut off by Islamic State, how do you feel?"

"How would anyone feel?" he replied glibly. "You can't judge a religion by its works."

I wish I had challenged that statement. The more I think about it, the more it sounds like a cop-out.

Of course we judge a religion by its works. When the Catholics, the Anglicans, the Salvation Army—as well as various government agencies—have been nailed for sexually abusing kids in their care, we don't let them get away with statements like "Don't judge us by our works." Of course we judge them that way. And if those works have been bad, we expect them to admit it and show penitence and responsibility.

❋

We are on the way home, Janna at the wheel. "What do you think?" she says.

"Small world," I say.

"Oᴋ, who did you meet?"

"Do you remember that young Uighur bloke who came to us in Islamabad?"

"Ah, yes. Tall lad. On the run from Western China."

"That's right. He was caught up in the protests against the Chinese squeezing their Islamic culture."

"And you helped him fill in papers to get to Australia."

"That's him. Abdurahman."

"Wow! You met *him?*"

"No, but his friend was there. Very nice guy. Somehow it clicked that we both know Abdurahman. They live in neighbouring streets, right here in Adelaide. I asked him to pass on my very best salaams."

Janna is shaking her head. "Grant Lock! Who will you meet next?"

We travel in silence for a few kilometres, then I speak up. "I did meet another interesting young guy today. He kind of shocked me."

"Shocked you?"

I share my encounter with Young Lawrence. She almost runs a red light. "Where is he getting that stuff from?"

I shrug my shoulders. "Maybe internet preachers. Maybe Facebook. I don't know."

"He might be in a cell or something, Grant. Are you going to report it to someone?"

I stare straight ahead and don't reply.

As we pull into our drive, Janna presses her point. "Islamic State is telling individual Muslims to rise up wherever they are. If something did happen you could be responsible, by not speaking up."

I click open my door. "You're right. I'll go down to the police station tomorrow." I turn my head and direct my imperfect gaze in her direction. "Providing I can find a woman a few years younger than me who will take me for a spin."

Janna rolls her eyes.

TWENTY-FOUR

DOUBLE DILEMMA

ADELAIDE, JANUARY 1959

"Ladies and gentlemen of Adelaide, you have seen two great singles matches, but the weather is …"

There's a flash and a crash, and the pungent odour of ozone fills the open-air stadium. The broad American drawl resumes. "I regret to tell you that we will have to postpone the doubles. You are invited to come back tomorrow at 2.00 pm."

The voice belongs to Jack Kramer, Wimbledon champion and tennis entrepreneur.

The next day is Monday. There are a lot of vacant seats at the Norwood Stadium as the champions warm up for the postponed doubles match. They are hitting up and chasing their own tennis balls. Dad turns to his fifteen-year-old twin sons. "Look, fellas, the ball-boys are all back at school. Why don't you two go down and help?"

Next thing Barry and I are in this magical arena, one at each end of the court, listening to the best players in the world connive and curse as they fight it out for Jack's prize-money.

Back in our hotel room, Dad is even more pumped than we are. The door is hardly closed when he announces, "I've got a plan, boys."

We wait, perched on the edge of the beds. The last time he said that, we built our own tennis court.

"Boys, I want you to become professional tennis players."

We gulp. Deep down, we would love to emulate our cat-gut swinging heroes.

Dad is still talking. "You can use your Commonwealth scholarships to study in the city. I'll find a top coach. I reckon you can go a long way." He turns toward the door. "I'm going downstairs for a drink. Think about it, boys." He pauses. "You'll make your grandfather proud."

It is one of the few times he has ever mentioned "The Curly Comeback".

Barry and I stare at each other. I start to dream out loud.

"You know, Hoad and Rosewall are called Australia's 'Tennis Twins', but they're not even related. We could be the real thing!"

Barry purses his lips. "Do you think he's serious, Grant? What about the farm? Cousin John won't be helping forever, and Dad's been counting on us. Look," and he raises his palms, "we both know Dad lives his tennis through us. He'd have been a lot better player himself if he hadn't wrecked his back with all the heavy farm work after his father had that accident."

Silence. Then I say, "What about just one of us coming to Adelaide, and the other stays on the farm?"

Barry says nothing. We are identical twins and we both know that wouldn't work.

The door handle turns. Dad is in a merry mood. It's been hard work getting the harvest off and now it's time to unwind. "Well, what do you think, boys? I reckon you'll be the top players in the Kimba Club by next season—just think how far you'll go with a good city coach."

Silence.

Finally Barry speaks. "Dad, I've decided to join you and Mum in the farming business."

"Me too," I echo.

Dad's shoulders sag. He stares vacantly at the sauce-stained breakfast menu on the coffee table. The professional tennis phantoms slowly drift back into the clubhouse of his mind. He heaves a pragmatic sigh.

He raises his head and grins. "OK, boys, that's it then. Farming it is."

TWENTY-FIVE

OUT OF YOUR BRAIN

ADELAIDE, 2014

It used to be called shell-shock. The soldiers never talked about it. Who would understand? Who *could* understand, except your mates at the RSL? But even there, it's better to remember the good times and the mates you lost. Tough blokes don't talk about feelings.

We've seen it and heard about it from our troops coming back from Afghanistan. No surprise that some have PTSD: post-traumatic stress disorder.

They've dodged land-mines. *Will I still have legs tonight?*

They've frisked waistcoats that could be suicide vests.

They've moved through the crosshairs of Taliban snipers.

And every day they've searched the eyes of their Afghan army colleagues.

Is he the good friend and comrade I've been training for months? Or is he waiting for the right moment to open fire and earn a martyr's welcome in a virgin-populated paradise? Have we done something that offends his honour, something that makes him quietly burn for revenge? You look into their eyes but you can never tell.

Green-on-blue violence they call it. Like when an Afghan soldier opened up on his Aussie mentors in August 2012.

At the end of a hot day, the diggers were unwinding, playing cards and chatting. The next minute, three lay dead and two more injured on Australia's worst day in the Afghan war. That incident should never have happened. It was revenge for the burning of copies of the Quran by American soldiers.

Who could you trust after that? Like the flames rising from the holy books, the PTSD graph was about to leap skyward.

I couldn't believe the Americans made such a mistake. Every foreign service person, from the chief of staff to the cook, should have been drilled on the culture and values of Afghans, particularly their respect for the Quran. After twenty-four years in Pakistan and Afghanistan, all I can say is that it was totally preventable. That powder keg of vengeance should never have reached the flames.

"It's only a book, Grant," my mate George says when we meet for coffee. "Surely they could be excused for burning them along with the other books." He adjusts his chair. "Weren't the prisoners at Bagram using them to pass along messages? They could have been planning a Taliban bust-out."

We've put in our order and found a table. It's a coffee shop, but George always orders Earl Grey tea. I settle for a double-shot mocha.

"For one thing, George," I counter, "the Quran is easily distinguishable by its decorated cover. And it's so significant to the locals, even if most of them can't understand Arabic."

"Well, what can you do?" George mumbles in a "that's life" sort of tone.

But I'm barely warming up. I don't even acknowledge the waiter delivering our beverages.

"I know what *I* would do! If I was in the training department of the military, I'd set three things in front of every new group of service personnel who arrived in Afghanistan."

George looks up from stirring his Earl Grey. "And what would they be?"

"On a table I would lay a grenade, a bottle of anthrax and a Quran. Then I would say, 'Tell me, which of these will give you the most trouble if you mistreat it?' And after they had thought about it, I would point to the Quran and say, 'This will be the most dangerous if you don't show it respect. That's just the way it is.'"

George scoffs. "That's a bit over the top. Weren't those American soldiers just following orders? They had no idea what they were burning. Those books meant nothing to them."

"That's my point, George," I say as we push back on our chairs and depart.

※

George is right. Those books meant nothing to the American soldiers. As a result we heard a lot more about green-on-blue revenge. I felt so strongly about it that I wrote a partly fictional piece and sent it to an Australian national newspaper.

IGNORANCE ON FIRE

Emulating Tom Cruise, the insurgent dangles above the heavy glass case in the National Archives building in Washington. There are three irreplaceable documents stored there. But the only one he wants is the sheepskin parchment. It's under that glass, safe forever in its atmosphere of argon, in a constant humidity of forty percent.

He smirks and activates his anti-alarm device. It was developed by Mossad and smuggled out by a Palestinian sympathiser. Those Jewish technicians are smart. There are only four of these in the world and they all do the same thing. They deactivate any currently installed surveillance system, anywhere on the globe.

A miniature diamond saw splits the glass. In minutes, he is out through the ceiling cavity. Inside his jacket is the document which, for Mr and Mrs Citizen of the United States of America, is more precious than any other.

That was yesterday. Today, the reaction of the Administration is on par with the fateful morning when the Twin Towers collapsed into a smoking pile of rubble.

"Quick, Chief! Look at this!"

The head of the CIA joins the stunned circle staring at a wall of monitors.

"They're burning it, Chief. That rotten bunch is burning the Constitution of the United States—the *original copy!*"

The chief's face darkens. "Don't they have any respect? So ignorant! They haven't a clue what this means to the American people." His jaw tightens. "They'll pay for this—pay for it with their blood."

Fists pump in unison. "Damn right they will!"

And on a freezing February day in Afghanistan, the word gets out in snow-bound Kabul.

"Quick, Chief! Look at this!"

The head of the Taliban cell joins the stunned circle of turbans staring at a Tolo TV News broadcast. "They have burned the Quran, Chief. Those infidel Americans have burnt our holy book." Bearded faces darken. "Don't they have any respect? So ignorant! They haven't a clue what this means to the Afghan people."

Jaws tighten. "They will pay for this," growls the Mullah, "pay for it with their blood."

Fists pump in unison. *"Allah O Akbar!"*

※

My story would have made little difference to the world views of the West. But one thing I know: if those one hundred Qurans had not been burnt, the payback at our Australian post in Uruzgan would not have happened. And fewer of our troops would have come home carrying the seeds of post-traumatic stress.

But things are changing. Stigma is declining, and society no longer turns a blind eye to the invisible diseases of stress. That's right: stress disorders are not a phantom of the mind, a weakness of the personality or a bout of nerves. Just like diabetes, arthritis or my macular degeneration, it's a disease. We are finally calling a spade a spade.

Now we have Mental Health Week. Medicos talk about it. Researchers are discovering new things. The media highlights it. Politicians are making speeches. And we are reminded that half of us, at one time or another, will experience mental health challenges. I am glad that, back in Afghanistan, our former organisation is establishing primary mental health care centres across the country.

"Cancer" used to be the hush-hush C-word, but now we can talk about it. Mental health is going through the same liberation. We no longer whisper "shell-shocked". "Stress-related", "panic attacks", "depression", "anxiety", "post-traumatic stress disorder": these are all words we

are familiar with today. And there are new words, too, like "brain plasticity" and "rewiring the neurones".
At last we are telling it like it is.

※

Whether it is a one-on-one conversation or speaking at a conference, Janna gets excited about the new discoveries concerning the brain. "They used to say that when the brain was damaged by things like PTSD, it was permanent." She waves her hands around. "It's not true! They've found that the brain is flexible enough to be repaired. That's why they call it brain plasticity."

"But how?" someone always asks.

Janna fills them in. "Along with up-to-date counselling, one of the key processes is to recite a series of sentences every day. But," she adds, "it has to be out loud and really fast. It helps the brain to repair itself, to rewire the damaged areas."

There are noises from the listeners.

"That's amazing."

"Never heard of that before."

"How do I find out more?"

Janna recommends good books on the subject, then continues, "Look! I still have some down days, and you have to keep working on it. But it's been a breakthrough for me."

Recently Janna spoke at a women's meeting. It was out in the sticks, at Walpeup in Victoria's Central Mallee. I can tell you that, whether it's country or city, when my gutsy, compassionate wife shares her story, women forget the time. They are lost in another world, another place.

Finally, when they stopped for a cuppa, a greying woman approached my wife and hugged her. "Thank you, thank you, Janna. For sharing about your stress attacks, and how you made use of medication to help you through." She brushes away a tear. "I always thought it was just me."

Janna returns the hug. "You're welcome. And I'll probably need that help for the rest of my life, along with the new things we're learning."

She squeezes the woman's hands. "It's all a part of God's healing and coping gift."

RECOMMENDED READING

The Brain That Changes Itself and *The Brain's Way of Healing* by Norman Doidge.

How to Switch On Your Brain and *Who Switched Off My Brain?* by Caroline Leaf.

TWENTY-SIX

THE PACKAGE

ISLAMABAD, 2000

"You are a good man, Ali. A man I can trust."

The pilot fingers the braid of the officer's cap resting on his knees. *"Jhi Janaab.* Thank you, Sir."

"That's why I promoted you last year; chose you above the others."

Ali has heard about the suave, suited man sitting behind that desk. You can always tell a Pakistani man's position by the size of his desk, and this one is huge.

Sadiq Sahib slides open the top drawer. "You are a man who respects your superiors, Ali, and always obeys orders."

Ali knows that he is not being buttered up for nothing. This is Pakistan, and there is always a time to pay back a favour: a better examination result, a blind eye at the customs counter, a promotion.

His boss reaches into the drawer and places a large packet on the desktop.

It's a plain parcel, wrapped in green plastic with a lot of tape. It looks ordinary enough, but they both know what is in it. They both know that, if a pilot carries it to Europe, it will elude the sniffer dogs and customs officials.

"Your next flight to Frankfurt is Wednesday morning."

The pilot nods.

"I'd like you to deliver this little package to our German office."

Ali feels the beads of perspiration gathering on his forehead. He's worked hard for his position. Thousands of hours flying all over the globe, including to Maria's Italy. It will all be over if he says no.

It's not the first time his boss has detected reluctance in a young pilot, but they all come round in the end.

The package goes back into the drawer.

"Think it over. Let me know on Monday."

The pilot rises, salutes the Savile Row suit and moves to the door.

"And Ali, I haven't seen you at the mosque lately. Is everything OK?" Sadiq Sahib doesn't wait for an answer. "I'll see you next Monday, and *choop karo*—say nothing."

※

Maria was beautiful, and she knew it. Ali couldn't take his eyes off her. It was mutual. It is hard to imagine a more handsome specimen than a well-educated, self-assured Pakistani pilot, with his immaculately trimmed moustache and perfectly pressed uniform.

It didn't really matter that he was a Muslim and she was a Catholic. "Sure," he told her one Sunday when she was showing him the fountains of Rome, "I go to the mosque for Eid ul-Fitre and Eid ul-Azre. But that's all."

"Same as me," she said. "Christmas and Easter keeps the family happy."

Italians are family-minded people, as are Pakistanis. So it should have all worked out. But different cultural backgrounds can put enormous pressure on a couple, even when they are deeply in love.

Maria expected a place of their own. Ali assumed she would be happy moving in with the extended family in Lahore. That's what all Pakistani brides do. But Maria pined for her own place—she didn't care how small.

She resented, too, being relegated to virtual servant status. Ali's mother could be charming, with gold dripping from her ears and wrists, insisting that guests try another *jelaabee* or another serve of lamb *qorma*. But it was Maria who had to clean up afterwards. Her three sisters-in-law were well up the pecking order. Hadn't they all produced sons? And they all spoke both Urdu and English. Maria could only communicate in English. No one here spoke Italian, and she struggled with the rudiments of hard-sounding Urdu, the everyday language of the community.

Maria felt trapped. Where was the freedom she had enjoyed as a woman in Europe? It wasn't that she hated the *chaddar*. It was the legalism. "Don't forget to cover your head when you are out, Maria," her female in-laws regularly reminded her. "You are bringing shame on our family and on your husband."

She found it best to say nothing, but inside, Maria burned.

Shame! Shame! That's all you think about! Mamma mia! Don't you know I was a free woman in Italy? I was in charge of a department in the travel agency. I went where I liked, when I liked! And I wore what I liked.

When little Ishaaq came along, they all said, "*Moobarak ho!* Congratulations! A son. You have brought great honour to Ali." But Ali was away days and weeks at a time.

Whenever she could, Maria took refuge in the bedroom that had been allotted to her and Ali. But never for long. There would be three sharp taps on the door.

Tap, tap, tap! "Time for you to clean the rice, Maria!"

Tap, tap, tap! "Bring in the washing, Maria!"

Tap, tap, tap! "We're going to the women's bazaar to buy gifts for our guests. Be sure to prepare the chicken for the *biryani*, Maria!"

Ali tried to console her. He was more moderate than the rest of the family. He had travelled widely and understood where Maria was coming from. He too felt trapped. He was glad when his flights kept him away on Fridays. Then he didn't have to front up at the mosque to preserve the family's honour. After all, his father was an influential businessman, a "somebody". Not to join him at the mosque just wasn't to be considered.

Ali could see what was happening, but what could he do? He was bound to his family, his clan and this culture of shame and honour. Instead of just going through the motions at the mosque, he started looking for answers; he started praying. And locked in her room, weeping, Maria also started pleading with her namesake.

But neither the prayers in the room nor the prayers in the mosque produced anything. No meaning. No response. Nothing.

"There is no God," Ali pronounced. "We are both praying, and there is no answer. No answer from Allah and no answer from Mary and Jesus."

They sat in silence. Then Maria whispered, "If you are out there, God—if you exist—please help us. Please show yourself."

And Ali said, "Ameen."

Little Sabina's arrival was hardly noticed. After all, she wasn't a boy. But Ali loved her big brown eyes. They sparkled like her mother's used to.

※

Ali can hear the train in the distance. It has all been too much. Things are not working out. *Better to end it all. Maria and the kids will go back to Italy. She will be happy back there.*

He lays his body on the track and grips the far side rail. He's chosen this place well. With the curve of the line and the summer darkness, the driver will not see him until it's too late.

He hears the rumbling clatter through the metal of the rails: *Better this way. Better this way. Better this way.*

A hand touches his shoulder. "*Bhai Jhi*—Dear brother." The voice is firm and strong. "What are you doing?"

Ali doesn't move.

"*Aa-o. Chai meraysaat pio*—Come, drink tea with me. Come, Ali, come!"

But Ali is consumed by the call of the rails.

Better this way. Better this way. BETTER THIS WAY.

TWENTY-SEVEN

THE MAN

ISLAMABAD, 2000

The train charges into the curve.

Ali stirs.

The voice, like the grip on his shoulder, is insistent, reassuring. "Come, Ali, come!"

The pilot slowly looks up and reaches for the man's hand. He rises. The hand pulls. The train carriages hurtle by.

ANOTHER DAY. ANOTHER DAY. *Another day.*

Up the embankment, through the bushes and over the road, the man leads Ali to a seat in a grotty chai shop. *"Doh cup subsay utchar chai,"* he says to the waiter with the grimy towel draped over his forearm. "Bring two cups of your very best tea."

The man talks. Ali has tears in his eyes. He has never heard words like these. "He who seeks will find, Ali," he says. "Seek with all your heart and you will find peace."

Another train screams past. Only moments ago Ali had wanted to become one with that scream. Now it's different. Ali stares at the man. "Sir, how did you know my name? Who *are* you?"

"I am a messenger."

"A messenger?"

The man does not smile, yet his whole face is a smile.

"You say I will find peace. Where? Tell me where!"

"In the words of Isa. Read his book. Read the Injil."

The train whistle blasts again. Ali glances toward the sound, then turns back.

The man is gone.

※

Red-eyed Maria does not understand. The uniformed husband who had hugged her and the children extra tightly when he left has returned.

But he is different. His shoulders are square, and there is warmth in his eyes and excitement in his voice.

"Maria, do you have an Injil?"

She looks puzzled.

"You call it the New Testament. The man told me to read it."

"What man?"

"The man who saved me. The man who pulled me off the train track."

Maria's hand goes to her mouth.

Ali embraces her. "It's going to be all right, Maria. Now tell me, do you have that book?"

"My grandmother gave me one, bound in leather. I've never read it, but I've always kept it."

"Good. We will read it together." He pulls up a chair. "But first, let me tell you about the man." He quickly relates the story. "And then, Maria, he just disappeared!"

His wife gasps. "Ali, you have found your angel!" Her face lightens. "Now I must find mine."

✻

The family protests when Ali tells them about the transfer to Islamabad. But he seems stronger, more confident and self-assured these days.

His mother daggers a look toward Maria. "What about the children, Ali? Without us, who will bring them up properly?"

"We'll manage," Ali says, ignoring the implications of the question.

"But Ishaaq must go to Aitchison College. All of our men have gone to Aitchison, for four generations!"

"Lahore is not the only place with good schools, Mother."

Ali's father refuses even to look at his Western daughter-in-law. She is not the cousin the family had chosen. She is the outsider, the one who refused to say the *Shahada,* who refused to become a Muslim after tricking his son into marriage. "Be very sure to find a good mosque, my son," he says. Ali's three brothers make supportive noises. The sisters-in-law sit in tight-lipped silence. They are losing their Cinderella.

Maria is excited, but she dare not show it. She won't have to put up with all the pecking and crowing from the higher perches. Perhaps in the capital her prayers will be answered.

※

In Islamabad, Janna and I are living in G10, the south-west part of the capital. Unknown to us, Ali and Maria have settled into an upstairs flat just down the road. Released from the burden of family control, they blossom. It is a long taxi haul to the airport, which is closer to Rawalpindi, but Ali is again enjoying his work. And as he reads the Injil, Isa Masih is answering his questions.

Maria has found a good kindergarten for Ishaaq and new friends among the wives of the Italian Embassy staff. They have told her where to find her favourite Ascolana olives, down at Melody Market. The problem is, they are always on the top shelf.

Unlike the West's monolithic mega-bars of merchandise, the supermarkets of Islamabad are small, with very high shelves.

"Oh, thank you," says Maria as she lowers her arm and her heels. "Thank you so much." The tall, fair-haired woman passes her the jar. "You are welcome," she says in Scandinavian English. "I come here all the time, but I have not seen you in Melody before. And your daughter is about the same age as mine."

The two-year-olds are already reciprocating the interest which little people invariably have in others their own size.

The mothers stop and chat.

※

It's been a heavy week for Ali in Seattle, training for the new Boeings. He dumps his bags, hugs his wife and checks on the kids in their beds. With a fresh cup of coffee in his hand, he starts to perk up.

Maria doesn't need the coffee. She perches alongside him on the sofa.

"Ali, listen! I have found my angel, and she is not the kind that disappears!"

Ali smiles. He always knew she would.

"I met her in the supermarket. Her husband consults for a power company. She's invited me to her group."

Ali nods.

"Yesterday, I went to her house in F7 sector, up by the hills. It was so good! We all talked, and they prayed for each other … and they read the Injil, like we do."

※

Outside our gate, Janna is sharing a carton of bar soap with women and girls in tatty clothing. The rush is soon over and the women depart with heavy, cloth-bound bundles of grass balanced on their heads. Janna notices another woman, who has been watching from a distance. She is wearing a local *shalwar kamiz,* but not in quite the way the locals do.

The woman moves closer. "Who are they?" she asks.

"Afghan refugees. They live out of town. They cut grass for their goats wherever they can. My name is Janna. If you have time for a cup of tea, I'll tell you about them."

And that is our introduction to the new family up the road.

On our second visit to their upstairs flat, we savour the aroma of Maria's Ascolana olive pizza in the stairwell. *Mmmm!* But at the meal table, they are visibly unsettled. It's something to do with a meeting Ali has with his boss on Monday.

Something to do with a delivery to Frankfurt next week.

TWENTY-EIGHT

THE DELIVERY

ISLAMABAD, 2000

Monday arrives. Ali dresses slowly. This could be the last day he wears his uniform. On his way, he again rehearses his answer:
Janaab, Sir, I am honoured to be a pilot in the airline. You have always treated me well. Given me opportunities to advance. I am in your debt forever. And, Sir, I know you are a person who always respects every letter of the international aviation law. You have set us the highest example. It would not be good to bring our respected international airline into dishonour. Perhaps you should reconsider.

He knows he could be more direct, but Pakistanis are masters of the honourable reply. He can see Sadiq Sahib's jaw tighten. He can see the parcel being pushed toward him, hear the boss saying, "Ali, you are the one who should reconsider." And he can feel his arms trembling, hear himself saying:

With respect, Sadiq Sahib, I am sorry, but I cannot take your parcel of heroin into Europe. It is simply not right. I have prayed about it—prayed about it a lot. And the answer is clear. I simply cannot do it.

He pushes through the doors at the entrance of the building. Inside all seems normal. Farouq, the security guard, snaps his heels and salutes. There are lines of customers at the ticket sales counters. In the corner air freight department, a fat man with a lot of boxes is arguing for a discount. A tea-boy rushes past with a tray of cups and dented teapot. Ali follows him up the stairs.

The morning is cool, but perspiration trickles down the nape of his neck.

What will happen to Maria and the kids if I lose my job? Perhaps this is a big mistake. I'll tell him I will do it, but just this once. Yet, if I do it once, he will have me forever. Brand me as a trafficker. Blackmail me. If anyone listened to me, he'd just pay them off. And why was he asking about the mosque last week? Does he know something? Does he know I now secretly follow Isa Masih—Jesus the Christ?

The pilot arrows a prayer upwards. "No, Lord. You went all the way for me. Now I must go all the way for you. Even if it does cost me my job, land me in jail. I want to trust you, but I am weak. Help me."

Jamila, the secretary, is her usual cheery self. "Did you have a good weekend, Captain Ali?"

The pilot is not up for small talk. "Sadiq Sahib is expecting me."

"Well, you might be expecting to see him," she laughs, "but it is going to be quite difficult!"

"Difficult?"

"He is not here."

"Then when will he be in?"

"He won't be. He left for Lahore yesterday. Headquarters transferred him, without notice." She leans forward and gives a quiet smile. "I think it was a demotion, back to his old department."

Ali exhales and whispers, *"Khoodar kar Shookr*—Thanks be to God." He turns on his heel and leaves.

Jamila is wondering why the pilot walks out taller than when he walked in.

TWENTY-NINE

THE BASANT TRAP

ISLAMABAD, 2001

The Basant Spring Festival is celebrated throughout Pakistan. The five million population of Lahore swells with visitors and relatives, both from within the country and beyond. Winter is over. The trees are bursting with blossom. By night and by day tens of thousands of colourful paper kites fill the sky. Drums, trumpets, spotlights, food and family reunions. The most excitement comes when the champions line up for the major tournament. The strings of their finely balanced kites are carefully coated with ground glass. The aim is to scythe through the opponents' strings until only one kite remains.

To win, you have to lay a trap. You have to lure your adversary into thinking that all is well. Then you swoop in, cut off the way of escape and sever the connections.

The phone rings. Ali has just returned from a long haul from New York via Heathrow. It has been six peaceful months since Sadiq Sahib was transferred.

Maria answers. "Yes, Ali is here." She thrusts the phone toward her husband, whispers "It's your father" and proceeds to herd the children into the playroom.

"Father, it's so good to hear you. How is your health? How is all the family? How is dear mother?"

The two men trade the culturally scripted questions and responses.

"We miss you all so much, Ali. We want to invite you to come to Lahore for a week, for the Spring Festival."

"Thank you, Father, but I will be flat out with flights from Manchester. You know how people love to visit relatives at this time of year."

"Well, at least Maria and the children must come. They love the kites, and your mother says she is missing Maria so much. She insists they all come for Basant."

Ali hesitates. "You are right, Father. The children always love the sweets, and the excitement of the competitions." He tries to sound convincing. "And if my flights to Lahore work out, I will definitely stop over for a night."

"We insist, Ali. This time, your mother will not take no for an answer."

"Ok, Father. It sounds like an excellent idea."

The older man seems relieved and changes the subject. "And Ali, I met Sadiq Sahib at the mosque last week. You know, your former boss."

Ali's body stiffens. "Ah, yes. Please give him my best salaams, Father. How is he going, back in Lahore?"

"Fine, Ali, just fine. But he said he was concerned about you. Said you never seemed to be at the mosque on Fridays."

"I am on duty a lot, Father."

"I know, son, but it was good of him to be concerned. Now be sure to arrange for Maria and the children to come down for the festival."

"Yes, Father, I will attend to their travel arrangements right away."

Ali puts the phone down slowly and stares at his puzzled wife. "It's a trap, Maria. They want the children!"

Her face turns pale. "I won't go to Lahore. I won't take them."

Ali takes her by the shoulders. "Maria! They will just come up here and get them."

"They can't do that!"

"Yes, they can. And no one would stop them. Not the police, not the courts, no one. They know I am no longer a Muslim. They believe I have disgraced them. I have disgraced Islam and my country. I now call God my Father. To them, that is blasphemy."

"But, Ali, there are already Christians here in Pakistan. And they go to their churches."

"Maria, they were born as Christians. They did not convert. It was their great grandparents who converted."

"Well! That's what you have done, isn't it?"

"Yes, but they were not Muslims when they chose Christianity; they were Hindus. If you are a Muslim, like I was, you are not supposed to change. Islam is a one-way street." He tightens his jaw. "And I am positive that the family knows I am walking the other way."

"But how can you be so sure?"

"Maria, when have they ever said they wanted to see you? That's the give-away. You know how they were never happy that you did not convert when we married. Now they blame you for luring me out of Islam. It's a trap so they can bring the children up as Muslims, not *kafirs*. And I'm sure Sadiq Sahib is involved as well. He must think I had something to do with his demotion. And he hates you for 'influencing' me."

Maria's eyes burn. "I don't care what he thinks, Ali. They are not taking my children! *Mai! Mai!* Never! Never! There must be something we can do."

"There is only one way, but we have to act fast. Before the start of Basant."

Like the master kite-flyers, Ali plans to lull his opponents into thinking all is well … before they cut off his escape.

Don't look down on anyone
unless you are helping them up.
AFGHAN PROVERB

THIRTY

SADIQ SAHIB

ISLAMABAD, 2001

Ali's mind is racing. *Exit visa for Maria. Tickets. Timing. Bank accounts. Who can I trust?*

He has already decided on his plan, a plan he has kept in the back drawer of his mind since his parents visited Islamabad.

It was a tense time. Grandfather and Grandmother spoiling the children with sweets and ice cream and trying to wheedle information from them: "How is your school?" "Who are your friends?" "What books do you read?" "Why has your father not been to the mosque?" Maria even caught her mother-in-law snooping through her drawers. But the carefully hidden Bibles had not been discovered.

In the West, the presence of an alternative holy book such as the Hindu Bhagavad Gita, the Buddhist Tripitaka or a New Testament could just mean that the householder is exploring spiritual writings. But in most Islamic countries, their presence means that the householder has already rejected the faith and converted. In Pakistan, the law decrees that such a change deserves death or, if not death, a life lived out in a violent jail.

Ali could read the body language, the stiffness and the forced smiles.

After the farewells, he drew his wife aside. "They know, Maria! They know!"

※

The international pilot puts his plan into action. After the diversionary bookings have been made, he rings Lahore.

"Father, I have the tickets for Maria and the children. They will arrive the day before the festival starts."

"*Sharbaash*—Well done, my son! Your mother and I will meet them at the airport."

But Ali's father does not know that when the children disembark, it will not be at Lahore. It will be at an Italian airport, five-and-a-half thousand kilometres away.

A week later, Ali returns from a domestic run down to Karachi. After the kids are in bed, he hands Maria an envelope.

"Is this the tickets, Ali?"

He nods. "I had to wait till I was in Karachi. Too many of Sadiq Sahib's mates in the ticket office up here. They are for three seats on my regular flight to Rome. You will be going home, and the kids and I will apply for asylum." He frowns. "As long as Sadiq Sahib and my parents don't find out first."

"How would Sadiq Sahib know?"

"He has eyes and ears in every airport, Maria. And be sure you do not say anything to your family when you are on the phone."

"But can I ask my angel's group to pray? I am sure we can trust them."

Ali agrees. "We need all the prayer we can get."

He passes her another bulky envelope. "I've withdrawn all the money I could. It is in American dollars. We'll need it in Italy, or in case something goes wrong."

※

In Lahore, a computer operator from the international ticketing office knocks on Sadiq Sahib's door. He pushes a printout across the desk. "They are leaving the country, Sir. Heading for Rome, just as you thought."

Sadiq Sahib smiles and reaches for the phone. "My friend, they are not going to join you for Basant. Ali is smuggling the children out to Italy. Tomorrow night!"

Ali's father explodes. "I will not have my grandchildren raised by *kafirs*. They were born in Pakistan, and we will raise them as true Pakistanis, as Muslims. It is our duty to Allah. Let the woman go. We never want to see her again. When we have the children, Ali will come to his senses. Come back to his true family. Back to his true faith."

There is a pause. "You have your people in Islamabad, Sadiq Sahib. You must do something."

The Savile Row suit smiles. "*Fikre na karo*—Do not worry. You will get Ali's children. I will see to it ... personally."

※

Ali gets to the airport in time for the regular briefings and departure checks. The deception is working. Maria will arrive soon, and in thirteen hours his 747 will land in Rome.

Inside the airport entrance hall, all is noise and movement. Businessmen rush by with briefcases. Bewildered families orbit around heavy-laden trolleys. Babies cry. Unintelligible amplified messages boom from wall to wall.

In the middle of it all, Aakil, the cleaner, pushes his mop up and down the hall. He continually watches the door. A bent smile crosses his stubbly face. He paid a lot for this job, but today he will recoup some of his investment. His one metre-wide mop leaves a trail of streaks which guide him on his return run. He slows to avoid one of the countless trolley pushers, then speeds up to intercept his prey.

The airman pauses. Aakil stops directly in front of him. He speaks quietly.

"Captain Ali, someone is looking for your wife."

Ali freezes. "What was that?"

"An old friend of yours is looking for your wife, captain."

Ali tries to bluff. "My dear sweeper, she has many friends here in Islamabad."

Aakil, the son of Muhammad Aakil, flinches. He does not like being called a sweeper. That is the name reserved for the Christians, who traditionally clean toilets and streets and deal with dead animals, like their Hindu forefathers. No. He prefers the title of "janitor". The pilot will have to pay more for such disrespect.

"It is not one of her local friends, Captain." The janitor leans on the mop as if to proceed with his dirt-displacing task. As expected, a braided sleeve extends and a hand grabs his shoulder.

"Who is looking for my wife? Who?"

"Not just your wife, captain. Your children too!"

Ali tightens his grip and shouts over the echoing sound of a flight delay announcement. "Tell me, man! Who is it?"

Aakil smirks and rubs a thumb against a forefinger.

The pilot reaches for his wallet. Several notes slide into the grimy hand. It does not move until it receives several more.

Aakil leans towards the pilot. "It is your old friend … Sadiq Sahib."

Ali's eyeballs drill those of the informant. "How do you know?"

"I heard Sadiq Sahib giving orders to the officers in immigration." Aakil smirks again. "Of course, there is no need for them to know that I have spoken to you about this. I am a man who can be trusted, am I not?"

Ali responds with more notes. He strides off toward the staff rooms, pulling out his phone. His hand is shaking.

In the men's rest room, the phone dials out. He tries again. Perspiration is building on his brow. *Is she loading the taxi? Is she already on her way? Maria, where are you? Answer me! Answer your phone!*

THIRTY-ONE

CAT AND MOUSE

ISLAMABAD, 2001

The ringing stops. There is a tentative, "Hello. Ali, is that …?"
Ali interrupts. "Maria! Listen! Do *not* come to the airport. Do *not* come!"
"Don't come, Ali?"
"Sadiq Sahib is here. He will stop you in immigration and take the children. Do not come!"
"What do I do?"
Ishaaq tugs on his mother's *shalwar*. "Mummy! Did Grandpa *really* say he would give me two kites?"
"Shush, Ishaaq, shush. Ali! Tell me what to do."
"Leave the house. Do not go back. He knows where we live."
"Where can I go?"
"You have to hide for a few days, Maria." The pilot is fuming. *How stupid! How blind! Planned everything—without a backup.* "Take the money and try to fly with another airline. Try, er, try Lufthansa."
"But where, Ali? Where will I go?"
"I don't know, Maria."
"I know! I will go to my angel."
"Yes. Yes!"
"What about you, Ali?"
"I must carry on. I'll ask for asylum in Rome. I'll wait for you."
The door creaks. Two men enter the rest room, discussing the cricket.
"I have to go, Maria." He whispers, "God be with you. I love you."
"I love you too, Ali."
Her mobile clicks off.

✽

Ishaaq bursts into the room, "Mummy! Mummy! The taxi is here!" He bounces up and down. "I'm going to have *two* kites, Mummy! *Two* kites!"

Maria reaches for a small bag. "Maybe, Ishaaq, maybe. But now you can help me." She thrusts the bag into the boy's hands and reaches for the bigger ones. "Quickly, take this down to the taxi."

✻

The 747 gains speed. Ali pulls back on the controls. The giant bird rises, sweeps over the Margalla Hills and points its blunt beak toward Rome.

"Are you all right, Ali?" the co-pilot asks. "You look pretty pale."

"*Bilkul teek hoom,*" lies the pilot, "I'm fine, perfectly fine."

But his mind is on the missing occupants of three empty seats in the rear of economy class. Trust and doubt are duelling in his soul.

✻

Maria presses the doorbell. Little Sabina is whimpering in her arms. Ishaaq is having a noisy "no kite" meltdown. The old watchman wheels in the suitcases from the taxi parked outside the walls. Tears fill Maria's eyes.

Tall Anika opens the door, baulks for a moment, then stretches out her angel arms.

✻

Aakil, the janitor, goes home, happy with his day's work. But Sadiq Sahib is livid. He wastes no time in starting the search.

✻

Anika's trusted driver reports what he has heard on the grapevine. "A 5000 rupee reward is out there for the taxi driver who picked up the foreign woman and two children from G10. All he has to do, Memsahib, is to tell them where he dropped them off."

Anika's voice is firm. "Tell the watchman to speak to no one. And he is to keep the gates shut at all times."

Next day, her phone rings. The voice is mature and smooth. "Excuse me for bothering you, Ma'am. Some of our passengers missed the flight to Rome this week. We wish to pay a refund for the tickets. The airline apologises for any confusion, and we will personally deliver the refund. Do you have a woman by the name of Maria with you?"

"I am sorry, Sir, you must have the wrong number. There is no one by that name here."

Anika hangs up and breathes a sigh of relief. The little family has already been moved across town.

The next hostess receives a phone call. She moves the phone from her ear and beckons Maria to listen in. "Excuse me, Madam. I represent the Italian Embassy. We are seeking the whereabouts of an Italian woman and her two small children. We believe they may be in danger."

Maria's jaw drops. She shakes her head violently and steps away.

"I'm sorry, Sir," the hostess says. "We are unable to help you. Goodbye."

Maria slumps into a chair, her hands holding her head. "That was not the Italian Embassy," she whispers. "That was Ali's father! He must suspect I am here. But how does he know? How?"

The cat and mouse game continues. Maria is shuttled westward to Peshawar. After two more weeks of hiding and planning, they fly out to India. It is not where the cats expect the mice to flee.

※

The last we heard, Maria and the children had been reunited with Ali in Rome, and their request for asylum had been accepted. Perhaps Ishaaq and Sabina are growing up in the city where the two principal characters of the fifth book of their Injil are buried. Like Ali and Maria, they too had encounters with angels: the apostle Peter with the jail-cracking kind and the apostle Paul with the ship-wrecking, life-saving variety.

THIRTY-TWO

SILENT NIGHT

It's a silent night all right. But when you've just been told to get out of town, it's far too silent. Better if the wind was blowing or a storm rolling through. Then no one would hear if the gate creaked, a dog barked or a baby cried.

There's no choice though. The message came through loud and clear: "They are coming!"

Joe's hand is shaking as he lights the oil lamp. He packs his tools, hides the gold in his belt, saddles the donkey and dons his robe. It's cold out there.

In the glow of the lamp he looks down at his sleeping wife. Funny how things can change! A few months ago he was ready to get rid of her. Her abdomen could no longer hide the secret.

"Who was it?" he demanded.

"It was God," she said.

Joe rolled his eyes. "That's very convenient. I suppose God sent an angel to tell you to say that." Mary nodded, and that didn't help.

How could those eyes be so peaceful, so clear, when she has just betrayed me?

"Well, it's all over, Mary. I'm not marrying a woman who sleeps around, and crazy to boot. You could be stoned for this. I won't turn you in, but we're finished. It's over."

That was just before the first message came through.

"Get over it, Joe!" the Messenger said. "Marry the girl. She's telling the truth. The boy is the one promised. From now on you have a mission. Look after Mary, and look after the boy."

Joe listens to the regular rhythm of the girl's breathing, and ponders.

This trip back to my ancestral town: all to please some Roman tyrant. They sure keep the screws on us. Count each one so they know how many there are to squeeze. Then the baby, and then those excited shepherds, and then the scholars from way out east and their mind-blowing gifts. Now those strange-talking foreigners have saddled their camels and shot through, without telling Herod where we are. He told them he wanted to come and worship too. Not likely! The only one Herod worships is himself. Crawling to the Romans, building great edifices, keeping us all poor.

And now, another dream, another message: Herod wants the boy. I'll bet he does! You'd think a Jewish king would celebrate the arrival of the Promised One. But Herod isn't a real Jew. He's a fake. Gets rid of anyone who gets in his way. Wife, sons, mother-in-law—even got rid of the high priest. Drowned him at one of those palace parties. No one is safe from that madman.

Joe kneels, then whispers, "Wake up, Mary! Shhhh. Get your things, wrap up the boy. Herod's coming!"

It is a silent night all right. No dogs bark. No watchman stirs. Two hundred miles later, the refugee family will reach Egypt.

Back in Bethlehem, Herod's henchmen arrive. The night is no longer silent. The blood of baby boys stains the arms of wailing mothers. Not just the babies, but also the crawlers and toddlers and runners. "Make sure!" the megalomaniac rants. "Find every boy up to two years old. And get out into the countryside. They could be hiding in the hills."

> Days of terror.
> Nights of screaming pain.
> Not yet
> but the promised boy's blood
> will one day stain
> the hands of all the Herods of the universe.

A bird can fly only as far
as its wings can take it.
AFGHAN PROVERB

THIRTY-THREE

WILL THE REAL ISLAM PLEASE STAND UP?

ADELAIDE, 2014

I usher George into our living room. "What is it you wanted to see me about?"

He takes a seat. "It's all these beheadings going on with this Islamic State crowd."

"Yes?"

"Well, it's really stirred me up."

"And you want to ask me if Islam is a religion of peace or not."

My guest's eyes widen. "Yes. But how did you know?"

"Not hard, George." I run water into the electric kettle. "Most thinking Australians are asking the same question, but only in their heads. It's politically incorrect to ask it out loud."

"Well," says George, raising a palm to shoulder level, "I see Islamic State holding up heads on TV. I hear about Boko Haram burning down villages and carting away school girls in trucks. And I've just seen on the internet that the Taliban beheaded seventeen people. And now all this trouble in France. It just goes on and on."

"The usual, George? Earl Grey?"

He nods and keeps going. "They all bear the name of Islam and seem so proud of what they're doing. Shout *'Allah O Akbar!'* all the time. And yet back here, we're constantly told that Islam is a religion of peace. It doesn't make sense."

I fossick around for the Earl Grey. Finally, my peripheral vision picks up a familiar box. "I'm listening, George, keep going."

"It's not just Muslims who are telling us that, Grant. President Obama said it's a religion of peace. Prime Minister Cameron in England said it's a religion of peace. And our own politicians are saying it. But then we get all these things on the TV." He pauses and thrusts both hands toward me. "You're the guy who has spent years in Islamic countries …"

I deliver the Earl Grey. "Well, George, it's pretty complex."

He settles back into his chair. "Hah! Tell me about it."

"Firstly, George, Islam is made up of many groups. They're not a single united force, as some people think. You have the two major blocks: Sunni and Shia. They just don't trust each other. They happily throw grenades into each other's mosques. Then they're divided into all sorts of sub-groups. In fact, this Sunni–Shia division is a major contributor to the toxic situation in the Middle East. Their mutual hatred and culture of revenge fuels the fighting and hijacks peace-building. Keep an eye on Saudi Arabia leading the Sunni charge, and Iran doing the same for the Shias."

"Nice," says George. "What started that?"

"There was a big argument after Muhammad died about who should lead the Islamic empire. Some said it had to be a relative of Muhammad—that's the Shias. And some said the best person should be chosen, regardless of bloodlines—that's the Sunnis."

"And?"

"They had a big scrap in what is now Iraq. The Sunnis won and since then have always been the larger of the two major groups." I open the pantry door. "Janna has some Scotch Fingers around here somewhere."

"Which group does Islamic State belong to?"

"They're Sunni, George. That's why they take out Shias wherever they can."

"Yeah, I saw that on TV. Just lined them up and shot them."

"And the most prominent terrorist groups, like al-Qaeda, the Taliban and Boko Haram, are all Sunni. Have a Scotch Finger, George." I pass the biscuit tin. "But there is another big struggle going on in the international Islamic community."

George dunks his Scotch Finger. I try not to notice. I can't stand biscuit dunking. "And what's that?" he says.

"It's the struggle between the fundamentalists and the liberals. The fundamentalists say everything should be done just the way the Prophet Muhammad did it, including beheadings. The liberals don't agree. They are trying to make Islam fit into a modern world. But they are having a hard time of it."

George lifts the sodden Scotch Finger. I grimace. He deftly vacuums it into his mouth. "Mmmm. But when you see those heads on TV, Grant, do you think they are making any progress?"

"A bit," I say, "but they are fighting the very nature of traditional Islam. The conservatives are quick to remind them that they are forsaking the true religion."

"But everyone should be free to practise their own form of faith," George says, "or none at all."

I ignore the soggy crumbs swimming in his Earl Grey. "Well, that's the way we do it *here,* George. We can choose. And religion and state are separate. But Islam teaches that there is no separation between religion and state. It declares that Islam is the perfect system for all mankind, and should direct every aspect of people's lives: not just the spiritual, but in their homes, in their families, in their institutions, in their law courts, in what they eat, in what they wear, in who they marry. It's called sharia law."

George's jaw drops a little. "And what's the basis of this sharia law?"

"It varies a bit between Islamic groups, but basically it's built around the Quran and other religious writings that record the actions and sayings of the Prophet Muhammad back in the seventh century. Groups like Islamic State are trying to restore their ancient empire operating on sharia law. And they are telling all Muslims around the globe that they should rise up and support them."

"From what I see of Islamic State," says George, "this sharia law is terrible. They go into non-Muslim towns, take the men out and shoot them, and then cart the women and girls off to use them or sell them. That's apart from the beheadings they gloat about."

"You're right. But Islamic State, like the Taliban, say they are only practising true Islam, because it's all written down in sharia law. Now the liberals can try and interpret it differently, and I wish them all success, but it is hard going for them."

"Well, if they don't favour that hard-line stuff, Grant, why don't they jump and scream that it's not real Islam?"

"Three things there, George. Many of them *are* doing that, but it's very hard to catch the media's attention. Severed heads and shooting up schools are more sensational and get more viewers, more advertising dollars. Secondly, the liberal Muslims are told by the Islamists—sometimes with threats—that they are not following true Islam. And thirdly, many just want to get on in life and not get involved."

"Ok," says George, "that's all very well, but you haven't answered my basic question. Is Islam really a religion of peace or isn't it? After twenty-four years in Islamic countries, you must have come to some conclusions."

I pause and squirm a bit.

"Well?"

"I might be called Islamophobic for it, George, but I find it hard to accept that traditional Islam is a religion of peace, and I'll tell you why."

THIRTY-FOUR

THE CLUB

ADELAIDE, 2014

"First, let me ask *you* a question, George. Do you belong to any kind of club?"

"Sure. My tennis club. Play twice a week. Love it."

I'm super-envious. "Half your luck! I can't even see the ball these days. Now, what would happen if you decided to stop playing tennis and took up bowls?"

"What do you mean? I'd just leave the tennis club and join the bowls club."

"What if the tennis club said, 'You can't do that, George. Tennis is the greatest game and everyone should play it. In fact, whether they know it or not, tennis is ordained for everyone. So, you can't leave.'"

"Don't be silly, Grant."

"And then the tennis club president took you aside and said, "George, you'd have to be crazy to leave. Think of the huge disgrace you'd cause for our wonderful club and its great founder."

George sits upright in his chair. "I'd tell them where they could jump."

"And then the president said, "George, think about it first. And remember, if you don't change your mind, we'll have to see you as no better than all those others out there—those misguided lawn bowlers, decadent cricketers, uninformed quilters and unholy chess players. In fact, George, you know the ancient rules of our glorious club. If you leave … we'll have to kill you!"

George blows air through his lips. "Come on, Grant, that's ridiculous. I'd tell them to change their crazy rules."

"But what if the president said, "Well, yes, a few members are trying to do that, but the club constitution clearly says that to change the rules is against the rules."

George moves to the front of his lounge-chair. His voice has an indignant tone. I'm wondering if he thinks I am making this up or just want to hit Muslims below the belt.

"Are you *really* saying Islam is like that?"

I lean forward. "Settle down, George. You're the one who wanted to know what twenty-four years in Islamic countries has taught me. Now tell me, have you ever seen a trap yard on a cattle station?"

"Trap yard? No. I don't visit cattle stations. What's that got to do with it?"

"A trap yard is a perfect example of the way I've seen Islam at work over there."

He gives a permissive sort of grunt. "Ok. Tell me."

I settle back in my chair. "There used to be a time when they rounded up the cattle on horses. Then came motorbikes, and sometimes helicopters. But they have found a simpler way. They build a big yard around the water-trough with a gate on each side. The outlet gate is quite normal but the inlet gate is actually two gates shaped like a funnel. The cattle learn to squeeze through the narrow end—it springs open a bit as they push through. But then it closes back to half the width of a beast. It means they can't get back out that gate. So they drink and leave through a normal gate, which is open on the other side."

"I get it," says George. "You shut the outlet gate and they're trapped in the yard."

I nod. "In twenty-four hours, they will all be in there waiting for you. And that is what Islam is like. You can come in but you can't go out. Islam encourages people—and in some cases, like those kidnapped high-school girls in Nigeria, compels them—to come in. But once you're a Muslim, you're not allowed to leave. That's apostasy."

George's face still tells me he is finding it hard to believe my analogies. "We don't see that in Australia, Grant."

"That's because we have Australian law and not sharia law. But it's very different in most Muslim-majority countries."

"Really?"

"Yes. Let me tell you about Jasmina back in Kabul."

"Jasmina came knocking on our door one day. Janna invited her in. She had a ready smile, but her face showed she had been through a lot of stress. Janna found out that she was a fellow school teacher. 'If you are a teacher,' Janna said, 'why are you knocking on doors looking for stitching work?'

"'We were refugees in Pakistan,' Jasmina explained, 'and when we came back to Afghanistan, the government crossed my name off the teachers' registration list.'

"She said it was because they had become Christians and somehow the government had found out. So she had to support her family with sewing work.

"Janna asked her what her husband did.

"'Nothing,' she said. 'He sits at home all day. His male relatives and other Muslim men told him that they would shoot him if he ever left the house. That's because he left Islam.'"

George puts his cup down and stares at it for a bit. He used to be a teacher and I figure he is feeling for the black-listed educator. "Is that common, Grant?"

"I could tell you a lot of stories."

"But aren't those countries still kind of developing and influenced by their old tribal rules?"

"Some are, but this apostasy rule is deeply embedded in Islam. Even Google will tell you that. Just do a search for 'apostasy in Islam'. The major theological schools of Islam all agree on it. If you leave what they call the 'house of Islam' and join the 'house of war', you must be punished for disobedience and bringing dishonour. If not by death, then by removal of your property and family and by imprisonment."

"But I thought Islam gave you a choice. That's what I've heard Muslims say on TV."

"Yes. The Quran says, 'There is no compulsion in religion.' But that was early in Muhammad's career. Later, he said that those leaving Islam should be killed. And while the four major schools of Islam support that, I ask you, how can anyone say that Islam is a religion of peace?"

George gives a sigh. "Well, it's a good thing that doesn't affect us here in Australia."

"But that's where you're wrong, George."

"How?"

"Well, if the club rules say that those outside the club are substandard and worthy of punishment or even elimination if they don't conform, then it gives a big 'go ahead' signal to those members who are militant. And that's why they appear in shopping centres or wherever and pull out their guns and bombs. They think they have a mandate from the founder of the club and its rule makers."

"Bloody hell!" George mutters. "Big problems in the club."

"Complicated, isn't it? Some members try to tell us that all is sweet and those tough rules don't count. Then others, like many in Pakistan, rush out onto the streets to uphold them. And I've talked to Australian Muslim leaders who insist that sharia law in Islamic countries must be respected, and that includes punishing apostates with death."

George looks at his watch and rises quickly. "Whoa, look at the time!" At the door, he turns and raises his hands. "So why don't modern Muslims change the rules?"

"Hard to do, George, but some brave Islamic scholars are trying, and there are millions of peace-loving Muslims behind them. They are the ones we need to encourage."

George gives half a nod and shakes my hand. "Thanks for the Scotch Fingers. We need to talk some more."

THIRTY-FIVE

THE LAST STRAW

KIMBA, 1963

As soon as I saw his father, I knew he was going to be big. And one look at Helen, in her eighth month, confirmed it. It was a thousand-mile truck trip from New South Wales, but Helen's mother was with her and all went well. What we didn't know was that it was going to be a breech birth. Luckily, it didn't happen at night.

When I saw those hooves, I acted fast. A calf is supposed to be delivered diving out, front feet first. Back legs coming first means that the cord can be pinched and the calf can die, particularly if it's big.

With the nearest vet more than a hundred miles away, there was always the need for a competent local to assist with a difficult delivery. Before he moved to Queensland, Rob Kelly was the one we rang when a cow was in trouble. We called him Ned and he was top notch. I worked alongside him, and learnt a lot. Everyone knew I wasn't as good as Ned, but when he left the district I was the one to ring. It was heart-breaking when they left it too late. Not much fun delivering a dead calf, but at least you might save the mother.

※

The Gundibri Poll Shorthorn cattle stud, in our opinion, was the best in Australia. Every year Dad, Barry and I would punch our Volkswagen across the endless Hay Plain to attend their annual sale. Our Pregnant Pastie didn't look too impressive parked beside the Mercedes and the BMWs of some of the long-established breeders, but that didn't worry us. Our passion was to get the best and breed the best, not to drive expensive motor cars. When the bidding was finished, we usually had what we wanted.

"Bill, those boys of yours know more about my cattle than I do," old Doug Monroe of Gundibri told our father. Dad just smiled. He knew his twin sons spent hours poring over the sale catalogues, checking on blood lines and performance.

Gundibri Helen 20th was one of those outstanding cows, and she was mated to the massive Gundibri Supreme 3rd. As luck would have it, old Doug had also put her mother in the sale, so we bid up and bought her too. They were loaded on the truck together.

※

By the time I move Helen 20th into the yards, Barry has joined me with the equipment and a couple of gallons of lubricant. "Look at the size of those trotters!" I say as I attach the ropes. "We'll have to work fast."

The huge calf finally emerges in a slippery rush. He lays motionless on the ground. Not a movement. Not a flinch. We haven't worked fast enough.

I grab the ropes and start spinning the calf around. I'm leaning back against the fifty-kilo weight.

"We've gotta drain those lungs," I shout.

I spin, like a farmyard version of Torvill and Dean, till the head of the calf is at right angles to my body. Mucous fluid streams from his mouth and nose. I slow, and he bumps to the ground.

Not a snuffle. Not a flicker.

"I reckon we've lost him," Barry says.

"Maybe," I say as I reach through the rails and pluck a straw from a handy hay bale. It's an old timer's trick I learnt from Ned. I slip the straw up the supine calf's nostril, give it a gentle wiggle, then remove it. Nothing. I grab another straw and wiggle again. With a mighty blast, the calf sneezes. He raises his head and takes a deep draught of air.

Barry and I grin at each other.

Kimbolton Supreme would grow and grow till he weighed over a ton "in his working clothes". He was a great bull and sired top stock.

※

The stud beef cattle business is like a three-legged stool. Every leg has to be strong if you are going to succeed. First you have to breed them, then you have to feed them, and then you have to sell them. It doesn't matter if you have the best genetic material in the world and they are fed just right; if you don't get out and sell them, you go broke. So we were always looking for ideas for advertising our stud in the cattle journals of Australia.

Barry is flicking through an American cattle magazine. "Have a look at this advert, Grant," he says. "It's a photo of four kids sitting on the back of a bull."

"Pretty ordinary size bull," I say. "Our Supreme could eat him for lunch."

Barry looks at me and smiles slowly. "You're right, and you've just given me an idea." He reaches for the camera. "Grab your golf clubs, Grant, and ask Janna to meet us at the cattle yards in half an hour. We'll need someone to press the shutter."

Years later, in Pakistan, I show some young men the photo which became the most distinctive stud cattle logo in Australia.

Ali shakes his head. "It is not to be being the true photo, Mister Lock. It is to be the *nuckilee* photo—the fake."

"It is not *nuckilee*, Ali," I tell him. "It is genuine." And while they all gawp, I quickly add, "I should know: the guy standing on the back of the bull, swinging the golf club, is me."

A wise enemy
is better than
a foolish friend.
AFGHAN PROVERB

THIRTY-SIX

AND ONE THING MORE

KABUL, 2004

The first time I met Tom Little, I couldn't help noticing how intensely he was studying my wife's face. He leaned forward and looked into her eyes. *Who is this guy?*

He held his gaze, then reached into his pocket. "Let me adjust your glasses," he said. "They're not sitting correctly." He always carried a small pair of pliers in his pocket. He made the adjustment, bent the right bits and Janna said, "Thank you."

But Tom knew a lot more about optical stuff than just bending glasses frames. He'd been in Afghanistan for nearly thirty years. In that time he led the charge in training eye doctors and nurses. He trained opticians to design lenses. He taught technicians how to grind the glass to measurements. When he went back to a university in the States to earn more qualifications, he wasn't there long before they told him, "You already know more than we do."

Tom served the Afghan people regardless of the regime. King, communist, Russian, war-lord, Taliban and Karzai. In Taliban times he received tip-offs, and when the black-turbaned soldiers arrived to confiscate the eye hospital equipment, it was not there. It had all crawled over the back wall during the night.

Tom was passionate about meeting the needs of the Afghan people. But his passion operated within pragmatic boundaries. We found that out when we had our first meeting in Kabul.

After he had fixed Janna's glasses, he lowered his voice and addressed us like a good father speaking to his children.

"Grant and Janna, you've come to serve the Afghan people. You must take heed of all of our security measures. Someone from our security committee will radio every night, just to see that you are home and all is well. They will notify you if there is trouble, demonstrations or whatever, in any part of town so you can keep clear. Always take a different route when you walk to work, and go at a different time. If someone is planning a hijacking or kidnapping, that will confuse them. They like patterns. If the committee calls and tells you to work at home, do not leave the house. And always keep your mobile radio and mobile phone batteries well charged."

Janna looked a little pale, and I was shuffling a bit. We had security arrangements in Pakistan, but this was a different level altogether. But Tom had not quite finished. "One thing more," he said. "It will help you to serve the Afghan people better if you accept the fact that you may die here." He slipped his pliers back into his pocket and moved off to talk to other new members of the team.

Janna and I looked at each other. In the back of our minds we knew this was true, but Tom's security mantra had moved the reality of our new situation right to the forefront.

In August 2010 Tom received a message from the elders of a remote community in mountainous Nooristan. "Brother Tom, it has been a long time since you visited our unworthy village. Our people are very poor and have many needs. Please come back with a medical team and people who will help our eyes. But beware of the Taliban."

Tom was well aware of the Taliban strongholds in southern parts of the province called Nooristan, the "land of light". The name held special meaning for him. The eye hospitals that he and his colleagues pioneered bore the name "Noor Eye Hospitals"—Hospitals of Light. That August, his team of about a dozen medical and optical people would go the long way round and come in from the north.

One of the other members of that team was Dan Terry. Dan was not a medical person, but he had a deep understanding of Afghan culture and language. Like Tom, he was a long termer with a similar commitment. He had worked in countless villages in good times and bad. He met with the village elders, talked to the young men, planned community development projects, and in times of flood or earthquake worked tirelessly. He spent countless hours cross-legged on their carpets, drinking green tea, helping them plan ways to improve their communities. Sanitation, community development, basic medical care, literacy.

The team rendezvoused with members of the village in a rugged valley. Leaving their four-wheel drive vehicles, they followed their guides up the mountain trails. They trekked alongside the horses that helped carry equipment. After about ten long days of serving the mountain people, they trekked back again. Satisfied and weary, they climbed into their vehicles and pointed them back toward Kabul.

That's when they heard the shouts of *"Allah O Akbar!"*

Only one of the eleven survived the bullets—bullets of hate, bullets of blindness. He was the Muslim driver, who screamed out verses from the Quran.

Tom lived and died by his mantra, "You could die here." His brave wife Libby later received a hug from the President of the United States as he presented her with Tom's posthumous Medal of Freedom. Tom was already in the arms of a higher power.

Our organisation asked for written contributions for a memory book, which would be given to the two widows. This is what I sent.

※

> Tom,
> you told the newcomers,
> "Take due care,
> but once you accept the fact
> that you could die out here
> it makes it a whole lot easier."
> In the reality of that advice
> you washed so many feet,
> you co-healed so many eyes.
> For you to live was Christ.
> There is pain in the hearts of those you left
> who now remain to mourn
> and ask, "Why Lord? Why has he gone?"
> But the Potter speaks to us, his clay:
> "My friends,
> Tom is with me in paradise today.
> To die is gain.

And when my time for you is right,
you will also hear
my 'Well done, daughter. Well done, son,'
and together we will drink green tea
and enjoy the cardamom,
you, and Tom, and me."

Dan,
cross-legged on the floor
among your Afghan friends,
you loved nothing more
than sharing stories into the night
after a day of repairing this
or planning that
for the poor,
for those who are loved but hadn't heard.
And when they saw the way you served,
they saw the face of the Lord.

Grant Lock, for Janna and Grant. August 2010

※

Yes, hijacking is a way of life in those countries. And kidnapping is a well-established, income-generating industry. We were never direct victims, but some of our friends and colleagues were. Some came back and some didn't.

Back in Pakistan, our neighbours in Peshawar lost a brother for many months until money changed hands. When he returned, his dense black hair was as white as snow.

Then there was the case of Janna's boss, Bishop Alexander.

Janna had a real soft spot for the diminutive Pakistani man with thick, wire-framed glasses. He would welcome her each day and she would prepare her machine to write the countless letters he would dictate to her.

"Good morning, Jonah," the old man would say.

"Good morning," Janna would reply. "And I keep reminding you, Bishop Sahib, that my name is Janna, not Jonah."

The kindly leader, with the cares of a strife-torn province on his shoulders, would nod his head. "Ah yes, it's Janna, not Jonah. I forgot." Then he would reach for a pile of letters. "Shall we begin, Jonah?"

Janna finally accepted the fact that her name had long ago been thrown overboard from Bishop Alexander's memory boat.

But one morning, there was no work for the Bishop of Peshawar's secretary. The Church Office was an ant's nest of police uniforms, frantic officials, peons and priests, all running around in unproductive circles.

The flustered diocesan administrator rushed past Janna, "Bishop Sahib has been kidnapped!"

Somehow, the criminals had got past the security guard at the gates of the large church compound. They rang the doorbell of the Bishop's residence and spun a hard-luck story to his daughter.

"Please come in," she said.

"No, no," they said. "We will wait here for Bishop Sahib."

When Bishop Sahib shuffled to the door, they produced guns and took him away.

But this was to be a kidnap story with a difference.

In a house just outside town, two of the kidnappers were left to guard the victim. They were concerned that he was becoming listless and pale.

Then the little bishop spoke up. "I know you want money, but you have a major problem. I am God's person. So you are fighting against God."

The kidnappers looked on as the small man gazed at them through his thick glasses.

"And one thing more. I am a severe diabetic. If I do not have my proper medicine and my injections, I will die, and you will have nothing to trade with."

There was little response to the first statement, but the second sent them into a huddle. Kidnapping was one thing, but being hunted down for murder was another.

The leader finally stepped back and announced his decision. "It's getting dark. Untie him! Take him outside!"

In the courtyard he pointed to a bicycle. "Oᴋ, priest, get on that and ride back to town. And say nothing about us or it will be worse for your family!"

The machine was thrust into Bishop Alexander's hands and the gate was thrown open. But he did not mount. Slowly he turned to his captors and made another announcement: "I do not know how to ride a bicycle."

So, in the evening gloom, one of the kidnappers had to pedal the bike back into town, with the bespectacled bishop clinging on behind.

THIRTY-SEVEN

LAND-LOCKED AFGHANISTAN

KABUL, 2007

They draw the snow that gives life to summer pastures, irrigates valleys and fills wells. The mountains of Afghanistan are profuse, impressive and magnificent. But their beauty has a dark side. They also cut communication, promote distrust, slow education, stifle supplies, harbour terrorists and bury entire villages. Our organisation has many projects—medical, community development, micro-hydro and education. But in those mountains, progress can be slow.

❋

>In this land-locked island of earth
>there is no shortage of mountains.
>
>The spined dinosaurs spread their claws
>across the ancient clans,
>and after generations of war
>their stony grip on the desperate poor
>of a desperate land
>stays strong.
>
>How long, Lord? How long?
>My Spirit is brooding over this land, my son.
>
>Well, what is your plan?
>
>I passionately love each one.
>
>Then, can't you move a little faster, Lord?
>The sun is sinking low in the Afghan sky.

My son,
as my sweat seeps
from your servant pores,
it's not for you to ask
when
or how
or what will be.

But yours
is to serve
and gaze my way,
and trust the rest to me.

THIRTY-EIGHT

STOP PICKING ON US!

ADELAIDE, 2015

He is tall, quietly spoken and obviously well educated. Question time is underway, and I ask this moderate Muslim leader, "What would you like to say to Islamic State?"

His answer stuns me.

※

A few weeks before this meeting, Janna and I were invited to celebrate Australia Day at a mosque we hadn't visited before. While the speeches were made in the main part of the building, the women watched on a television screen in a separate room. Janna was a huge hit with the ladies. They found out she could speak some of their language.

"Where are you from?" Janna asked one particularly friendly Pakistani matron.

"From the Sindh. From a little town you would not have heard of."

"You might be surprised."

The woman rolled her well-covered head. "It is called Digri. Only small."

Janna's face lit up. "Digri! Of course I know it. It's on the edge of the desert where we worked. We always stopped in Digri to buy fresh naan. Then we wrapped it around bananas and drove on to Mithi."

The woman half leapt from her chair and called to her friends to come and meet this Adelaide woman who knew all about her home town.

But the world got even smaller when Shafiqa arrived. "Janna, don't you remember! You and Grant kindly came to our home for a meal when we arrived in Australia. I was so embarrassed. I was just learning English and I instructed my son to buy lettuce instead of cabbage." She laughs. "It was not a good curry."

After the formalities, I sat with the men around plates of delicious barbecued chicken tikkas. They were enthusiastic about their religion, and that's fine. But what I really liked was their enthusiasm to be part of Australian society and their rejection of Islamic terrorism.

"What Islamic State is doing," one Jinnah-capped leader said as he loaded more chicken kebabs onto my plate, "is a disgrace to Islam. We are totally against the use of violence."

I would soon be at another gathering where I would look forward to similar affirmations.

❉

The Islamic leader repeats my question. "What would I say to Islamic State?"

I nod, fully expecting a response similar to the statements made around the chicken tikka table.

"I have nothing to say to Islamic State," he says, stroking his neatly trimmed beard, "because Islamic State is not here."

I'm confused. *What does he mean? Here in this room? Here in Australia? But wait a minute—we know Islamic State is spreading its digital tentacles around the globe, and we know they reach into our country's phones and screens. We also know young Aussie men going to Iraq and Syria to fight with IS.*

My thoughts convert to speech. "But, Sir, since the emergence of Islamic State and other militant groups, many Australians are fearful and suspicious." There are affirming noises around the room. "They want to be assured that moderate Australian Muslims don't support that sort of thing."

There. Just in case he didn't understand the meaning behind my question, that should make it clear. Now he can reply and settle our minds.

But the leader does nothing of the sort. He responds in a different way.

"We do not have to keep answering this question," he says with an affronted tone. "We have been in Australia for many decades now. We have proven that we fit into this society. Why do people have to keep asking us this question?" He surveys the room. "Did you know that a recent poll shows that thirty percent of Australians hate Muslims?"

There is silence around the group. Somehow a feeling of guilt has snookered the conversation. But it hasn't snookered my brain.

Well, Mr Leader, now you've resorted to the "stop picking on us" approach. Somehow it seems like a politically clever way to derail responsible dialogue. I don't know if your hate-checking poll is accurate or not, and I'm sorry that you feel picked on. But you have to face up to the reality of the situation. If it was Rotary International that was holding up severed heads and carting away truckloads of women and girls, wouldn't we want to check on Rotary clubs and Rotary members back here?

I don't want to pick on anyone. But your implication is that there are no bad apples in your barrel. That's simplistic. There are bad apples in every barrel.

The silence lingers. The chairman rises, announces that question time is over and that we will break for supper.

While others line up at the tea and coffee urns, I manage to speak with the leader. "Sir, I am really worried. I too am concerned about our Australian Muslims. Surely it would be better for you to condemn the violence of Islamic State, and do it often, to help Australians to be supportive. I know there is a lot of good will out there. Don't you think you should build on it?"

He thanks me quietly for my concern but does not address my question. He shakes hands with a few others and then leaves.

On the way home I am still grappling with the issues.

Mr Leader, you spoke well and you are a convincing communicator. But I'm coming away with just the kind of suspicion I expected you to allay. I want to believe the best of you. Are you secretly happy about Islamic State and its plans for a new international Islamic caliphate? Are you one of those Muslims who are happy to see Islam grow under any circumstances? Or is it that your heavy-duty Eastern shame and honour thing, fortified by your Islamic teaching of superiority, prevents you from admitting there are problems in the Islamic world?

Of course it's not good that some people here show hatred to your Muslim brothers and sisters. But let's keep things in balance. You demand respect for Muslims here, but how much are you speaking out against the lack of respect given to non-Muslims in Islamic countries? And what about any of their citizens who move out of Islam? Tonight you told us that they should leave their Islamic country or be punished with death.

There is something incongruent going on here. Maybe I have misread your responses, but I certainly feel that you have misread the concerns and the fears of the Australian community.

THIRTY-NINE

MELONS

ADELAIDE, 2015

George is back. I didn't even notice the ring of the door chime. Janna has her own guests, so she shows him into my office.

I direct him to a comfortable chair and rotate my swivel chair towards him.

"You look stressed, Grant," he says. "A bit of writers block?"

"Sort of," I mumble.

He glances around. "Haven't been in here before." He looks over my shoulder. "Nice big computer monitor."

I give half a nod. I'm frustrated. I've been interrupted. When you've finally snared the thoughts flitting round your brain, you just want to get them into digital readability. "Er, yeah. I need it. Allows me to use what's left of my peripheral vision."

"If your central vision is all gone, how do you see the keys on your keyboard?"

"I touch-type."

The ideas in my brain butterfly off. George may be a bit rough around the edges, but he's a good friend. So I'll let them fly and net them again later. I tap in a couple of words and, as I do, a voice recites them back. That's my ZoomText screen reader. It reads back as I type, or later when I am editing.

"Great technology," he says. "So what are you working on?"

I tell him about the meeting with the Islamic leader, and about the unexpected turmoil I felt when I came away.

"You're not the only one," George says. "Yesterday I saw part of an interview with some Islamic preacher saying that Australia will one day have that sharia law you talked about. Then they interviewed a Muslim who lectures in a university and he said something different. That's why I came over."

"You need to know about the five faces, George."

He looks blank. "What five faces?"

Janna silently enters with an Earl Grey, a mocha and a bowl of mixed nuts. I'm pleased about the nuts. None of that biscuit-dunking and synchronised-slurping today!

"Well," I say, passing the tea to my visitor, "one observer of Islam, Dr John Azuma, who has a Muslim background, says that Islam has five faces and that it is not unusual for Muslims to wear more than one face at a time."

"Tell me about it," says George.

"The first is the spiritual face. We have to remember that over one-and-a-half billion people follow Islam as their religion.

"The second is the missionary face. All Muslims are supposed to take their superior message to the world. They call that *dawah*."

I pass the nuts to George. "And the third face?" he says as he slowly picks out all the cashews. I grimace. He's not the only one who likes cashews.

"That's the political face. Islam says that it has been shown to be the best, and the only, system for all humanity. There will be peace when everyone submits. Islam actually means 'submit.'"

George stops chewing. "Well, it shouldn't have to be at the point of a gun! Did you see that report from Syria on the news last night?"

"That's the fourth face. The militant face. The 'guns and God' face. Sometimes it's worn with the political and missionary faces. It is OK to use force to bring about God's perfect plan. This is the face worn by lslamic State, al-Qaeda, the Taliban, Boko Haram and many more."

George squeezes the nuts in his fist. "Makes me mad. They burnt that fourteen-year-old in Pakistan, just because he wasn't a Muslim."

I pause. Familiar faces flash onto my memory screen. "I get angry too, George. I've lost good friends to Taliban bullets. But it's no good taking it out on every Aussie Muslim we see, treating them like either terrorists or lepers."

"So what do you do?"

"Treat them like other Australians—or even *better* than other Australians, because they are really feeling the pressure. But," and I raise a finger, "at the same time we need to take the politically correct bandages off our eyes. Be informed. And beware of the two watermelons."

"Two watermelons?"

"It's an old Afghan proverb. 'You can't hold two watermelons in one hand.'"

"And what does that mean?"

"The political face wants separate laws for their religion." I can feel my blood pressure rising. "In England, people are wondering how they ever got parallel Islamic arbitration courts. I'd hate to be a woman trying to sort out family matters, divorce, property and custody of kids under sharia law. In most sharia courts, a woman's testimony is worth only half that of a man's. Muslim men can marry non-Muslim women, but Muslim women cannot marry non-Muslim men. A daughter receives half the inheritance of a son. A woman has no custody rights over her children over the age of about seven years."

I take a breath. "So our politicians should watch out for those who start pushing for that kind of thing here. We want one legal system for all Australians, not two."

"Now I get it," says my visitor. "You can't hold two legal watermelons in one hand."

"That's right. Despite claims to the contrary, Islam is very weak in human rights." I am on a roll and my arms are waving. "Show me a woman who can drive a car in Saudi Arabia. Show me a church building in Afghanistan. Show me someone in Pakistan who can leave Islam without personal danger or death."

"But surely they want to get past that stuff. Modern Muslims, I mean."

"I have no doubt that some do, George. But I guess you haven't heard of the CDHRI."

George looks mystified.

"The Cairo Declaration on Human Rights in Islam," I explain. "It was formulated in 1990 and supported by forty-five Islamic countries."

"Well, there you go, Grant! It looks like they *are* concerned about human rights after all."

"It certainly looks that way. And the Declaration says lots of wonderful things about freedom and rights. Until you get to the end. Then it says, 'All the rights and freedoms stipulated in this Declaration are subject to the Islamic Sharia.' Since sharia doesn't treat everyone equally under the law—and certainly not women, girls and unbelievers—where does that leave things?"

George shrugs. "Back at first base, I suppose."

"That's right. And it's a big challenge for Muslims who want moderation."

"Are our politicians awake to all of this, Grant?"

"Some are. And the rest could be, if they read something like this." I pick up a book from my desk. "It has contributions from a lot of international experts." I pass it to him. "It's an excellent read."

I feel him staring at me. "But you can't read, Grant!"

I chuckle. "I should have said it was a good listen." I gesture toward a small device on my desk. "I put it under this scanner and it reads it out to me."

"More technology," says George. He studies the cover. "Hmm. Looks interesting."

"Borrow it if you like. It brings out the low human rights values of Islam, talks about sharia law in Islamic countries, and discusses how some Western countries have been drawn into allowing parallel systems for Muslims, because Muslims say it is their democratic right to practise all aspects of their religion."

George ponders silently for a moment. "What about these young Islamic radicals who just show up and start shooting people, then say it's for Islamic State? The politicians have to do something about that."

"Absolutely. And they are working on it. But they need strong support and cooperation from our Muslim community. And it's not going to help if we marginalise every Muslim we meet. They need friendship, not hatred."

George slowly rubs his cheek. "It's all very confusing, though. One lot keeps saying they're all terrorists, and another lot keeps saying Islam is a religion of peace."

"The problem is, George, both can be afflicted with tunnel vision. They don't see the big picture. It seems they would rather be blind."

George thinks for a bit, then puckers his lips.

"Hmm. OK, but you haven't told me about the fifth face."

RECOMMENDED READING

Islam, Human Rights and Public Policy is edited by David Claydon and published by Acorn Press (2009).

In childhood you are playful,
in youth you are lustful,
in old age you are feeble.
So when will you
before God
be worshipful?
AFGHAN PROVERB

FORTY

THE FIFTH FACE

ADELAIDE, 2015

I grab some peanuts from the bottom of the bowl. George has eaten the rest.

"The fifth face is the progressive face. It's worn by moderates and liberals, who are taking a fresh look at the holy books. They reject force and are working to bring Islam into modernity."

"All power to them," George says.

"But the progressives meet with serious, sometimes violent, reactions from conservative Muslims, who see no room for change or amendment. The progressives can be labelled 'un-Islamic'. So it's a real struggle. Understandably, they don't want to be marginalised by the rest of their community."

I lean back and sip my mocha while George's brain processes the fifth face.

"Well, how many of these progressives do you think we have in Australia?"

"I don't know, but another expert on Islam reckons that up to sixty percent of Australian Muslims are not interested in the more serious faces. They just want to get on with their lives, get jobs, get their kids a good education and get a house if they can."

George laughs. "Sort of Christmas and Easter Muslims."

"Kind of. But regardless of the face, we should do our best to show friendliness toward them."

George purses his lips. "How do you do that, then?"

"It's not hard. You just have to look past the beards and the headcoverings. They are people, just like everyone else. Some have come from really tough situations and find it hard to adapt."

"What? Here in Australia?"

It's obvious my guest has never experienced culture shock. "Look, George, we have a great society, but let's not pretend it's perfect. When you come from a culture where the family decides who you will marry, and you never go out with others before or after, and males and females don't dance in the same room, then our culture can be seen as very loose. And when the female form is used to sell everything from ice cream to insurance, that doesn't help. Moreover, many are still grappling with learning English."

George is nodding slowly. I continue, "We have met lots of great Muslim people. Strong in hospitality. Love to have you come to their home, or to visit yours. And you'd be surprised how many haven't ever been invited into an Aussie home."

"Never thought of that," he says.

"Just be friendly. Say hello in the supermarket or wherever. And if you're a praying person, Muslims love to know you are praying for them. And by all means, exchange views about life, values and religion—you'll find things in common as well as differences. Be a learner."

George rises. "Well, it's all pretty involved. But I think I'm getting more of the big picture. The 'faces' and 'watermelons' help." He returns his empty cup to the tray. "But, you know, it's hard to talk about some of this stuff. People just say you shouldn't pick on Muslims. 'Show tolerance.'"

"I know. You have to be diplomatic. The problem is that words can change their meaning. What we need is a bit of good *old-fashioned* tolerance—the kind that says, "We may debate and disagree, but I will listen to your point of view and you will listen to mine, and we will respect each other." The new, politically correct version of tolerance says, "Show respect for others. Don't ask questions or express a point of view. That might offend someone. Just keep your mouth shut."

George laughs, then reaches into his bag. "Here's a little thank you for having me."

He hands me a packet of Scotch Fingers.

FORTY-ONE

NEVER SAY NEVER

ADELAIDE, 1965

The university students boarding in North Adelaide's Mary Seymour Hostel must be desperate for entertainment. Whenever a young suitor calls to take one of them out, the girls leave their study and quietly gather on the landing at the top of the stairs to assess the various qualities, or lack of them, of their visitor. In hushed tones, they compare notes on the fidgeting boredom-breaker waiting below.

In South Australia there is an acute shortage of home economics teachers. The Education Department has fast-forwarded its training program, and Maxine Janna Klaebe is working hard to keep up. It's Saturday morning, and her friends Leonie and Ginny are all dressed up. The hostel doorbell rings.

Maxine gathers with the others on the upstairs landing.

※

Maxine always wanted to be a teacher. Her greatest motivation came from an interview with the Quorn High School principal. He had been studying her academic results. Art, history, English, science, geography, home economics and physical education were all good. But mathematics was different. Maybe he had heard noises from Stocky French's maths classroom.

"Hell's bells, Maxine Klaebe! How long before you learn that the circumference of a circle is simply *pi* multiplied by the diameter?"

The recipient of the geometrical blast was the smallest in her class. There was no way she was going to vocalise her thoughts.

Pie? Pie? I know apple pie and wild peach pie. And I know magpies. But this "circle pie" thing is just useless gobbledygook.

The interview in the principal's office was brief. It was a kind of Jurassic precursor to modern vocational counselling.

"Now, Maxine, I think you should aim to be a shop assistant."

"But sir, I don't *want* to be a shop assistant. I want to be a school teacher."

He shows her to the door. "I think you will make a lovely little shop assistant, Maxine." He pats her on the shoulder. "The world needs shop assistants, you know."

And that was the moment that Maxine gritted her teeth and resolved that she *would* become a school teacher. She would do the hard yards. She would show them all.

※

It's Royal Adelaide Show time. Barry and I have driven five hundred kilometres from Kimba, the small town with the big sign-board, "Halfway Across Australia". We will attend the stud beef cattle judging, and we need to find dates for the Beef Breeders' Annual Ball. Barry has already invited Leonie, the tall, curly-haired daughter of a Yorke Peninsula cattle breeder.

But I have a problem. "Look, Barry, I've run out of leads. Do you think Leonie has a friend who'd like to make up the foursome?" It turns out that amiable Ginny is happy to join us at the judging as well as the ball.

The hostel's front door opens and a hush falls on the gaggle of girls kneeling behind the railing on the upstairs landing. As two young men enter, eyes bulge and the whispers begin.

"They're dressed exactly the same."

"They look like twins."

"And look at those hats!"

"With the funny little feathers in the bands!"

The spies are struggling to suppress their chuckles. Without a doubt, these guys are boredom-breakers of the highest calibre.

So here we are at Mary Seymour Hostel to escort the lovely pair to the cattle judging. Yesterday, we were shopping downtown and found some rather classy—well, *we* thought they were classy!—narrow brimmed, Bavarian felt hats.

We strut through the door to greet Leonie and Ginny. Fortunately, we are oblivious to the whispers and giggles upstairs.

As Maxine Janna chuckles at the identical duo from the bush, she turns to one of her friends and whispers, "You know what? I would never, ever marry a hayseed!"

※

Several years later, Maxine and one of those hayseeds find themselves on the same family mission team at Arno Bay. Our group of twenty has been running a variety of fun programs for the farming families who are taking a post-harvest break at the beach before their kids go back to school.

Over the last ten days I have been watching her dark-brown eyes and slender figure. Her strong alto voice and bursts of unpretentious exuberance attract me and her thoughtfulness and compassion arrest me. I am inspired by her contemplative faith.

I've been out with a lot of fine lasses, and I've had many fun-loaded double dates with my identical twin brother. On occasions, I've even competed with him for the attention of the same confused girl. The young ladies who attract me most are the ones with real depth of character. It also helps if they are good on the dance floor. Petite Maxine excels in both.

On the final day, before we head in opposite directions, I invite her to take a walk.

As we stroll along the town's long wooden jetty, she sticks close to me, then slips her arm around my waist. I like it, and I return the compliment. The sea breeze tosses the waves and tussles her dark hair. Her grip tightens and I feel her body lean into mine. I'm excited that she is signalling affection.

Years later, I'm recounting all this to her. She throws her head back and laughs.

"Affection, Grant? It was nothing of the sort! You know I can't stand being over water, on bridges and things like that. I held on to you because I was frightened, not because I was showing feelings for you!"

Perhaps it's my male ego but I don't believe her. On that Arno Bay jetty I saw an intense, wistful glow in her eyes.

In 1970 I proposed to Maxine Janna Klaebe. Eighteen months after the jetty walk, the home economics teacher married her stud cattle-breeding hayseed and our adventure began.

As we looked into each other's eyes and declared our vows, we never dreamed that this adventure would lead us on a life-challenging journey to the sand dunes of the Sindh, the tribal areas of the North-West Frontier and the land-mined mountains of Afghanistan. Or that one day I would return, half blind.

The diminutive dynamo from the Flinders Ranges has stood beside me through it all.

FORTY-TWO

THAT WOMAN

QUEENSLAND, 2013

It lasted all the way from South Australia to Queensland. There were many times I wished she wasn't with us.

Sybil was a pretty good sort, really. But when it came to travelling, we found that three can definitely be a crowd. She and her husband run a hotel, but this being the quiet winter season, Sybil was free. When she heard about our new car, she just had to come.

We'd been planning this road trip up the east coast for a while. Six months before, Janna said, "Let's see Queensland!"

I said, "Let's take up some *Shoot Me First* speaking invitations on the way."

"Good thing I like driving," said Janna.

I was envious. I really miss being behind the steering wheel. I miss the feeling of being free and in control. But with my dead-centre vision (with the emphasis on "dead"), I can't even navigate, let alone drive. Luckily, Sybil was happy to read the maps, so we loaded up the vehicle and off we went.

It wasn't long before Janna and Sybil were having words.

When you're together for six thousand kilometres, the good and the bad both come out. Sybil always had to be up front next to the driver. So I was relegated to sitting behind her. And she had this thing about speed. It nearly drove Janna mad. Sybil was checking the speedo all the time.

There we were, out in the middle of the Hay Plains without another vehicle in sight. The roads are long, straight and boring. Everyone knows you can creep up that extra four or five Ks and you won't get picked up.

But not Sybil.

I could feel the tension rising. Janna wanted to move along a bit, and Sybil was just waiting to jump at her with a serious reminder. "You are over the speed limit." There were a lot of arguments.

The nagging got Janna down. It wasn't only what Sybil said, but the know-all way she said it. Janna resorted to some pretty snappy responses.

"Ok! Ok! Give me a break! I'm only *just* over!"

"I am *not* over, Sybil! Didn't you see the sign?"

I didn't get involved. With my vision impairment, there was no way I could read the speedo or signs, so I couldn't say who was right and who was wrong.

After six weeks, we finally pulled back into our own garage. Janna gave a big sigh. "Glad to be home," she said, "and no more Sybil. All that nit-picking about speed. She was getting me down big time!"

"But she surely saved us money," I said.

"How is that?"

"Well, six thousand kilometres and no speeding fines. That's pretty good."

Janna pouted.

"And," I added, "she didn't eat much. And she had no complaints about sleeping in the car. That was another saving."

"She wasn't always right, though," Janna retorted. "There were plenty of times she said I was speeding, and I wasn't! She should have taken more notice of the speed limit signs. And what about when she got us lost near the Gold Coast? And then again down in Gippsland?"

I nodded. "You're right. When you're getting the car serviced next, you'll have to get them to download the latest GPS maps into her memory."

※

I can tell you this. When you have vision problems, you meet a lot of helpful women.

Apart from our GPS navigator, Sybil Fawlty, there is that lady who hangs out in our bathroom. First she says, "Please wait." Then she says, "Step on the scales, please." At least she uses her manners! That's more than I do when she reads out the increase in my weight.

Then there is the woman who is always beside me, hanging on my left arm. The grandkids love her. "What's the time, Grandpa?" And they rush up and press the button on my talking watch.

And there are a couple of helpful ladies who live in my Apple iPhone. Most people know about Siri. She takes my voice commands.

"Ring Janna's mobile."
"Wake me at 6.30 am."
"What's on tomorrow?"
"What's the capital of Somalia?"

But few know about the other woman, who helps me to do everything you can do on your smart phone, just a bit slower. Her unattractive name is 'Voice-over.'

Then there's the lady who lives in my ZoomText computer software. I am listening to her right now as I type.

It is love that makes possible
the impossible.

FORTY-THREE

MISCALCULATION 1

MOUNT RIDDOCK, NORTHERN TERRITORY, 22 JULY 1969

There are moments when you know that, without some outside intervention, you would be doomed. My nephew's sixteenth birthday in the centre of Australia was one of those times.

"John," I had announced the night before, "for your birthday, let's climb Mount Riddock."

"Sure, Uncle Grant. Have you ever done it before?"

I shook my head. "Never had time. Too many cattle breeders to visit. And we don't get up here very often."

John smiled. "Then I'll be your guide. We'll leave the homestead early, before it gets too hot."

So, next day, there we were, standing on the top of one of the highest ridges in the Hartz Range in Central Australia. We could see for miles. Shielding our eyes, we spotted a pair of wedge-tailed eagles circling high above. Far away on the Plenty Highway, dust clouds puffed up behind Matchbox series road-trains hauling cattle to the Alice Springs sale yards. On the way up, John showed me one of the places where the fossickers look for gems. We scraped around and found a couple of fairly ordinary garnets. I slipped them into my pocket and we continued to climb to the top.

After our 360-degree scan of the outback, John waved an arm. "Come on, Uncle Grant, it's time to toss some rocks. There's a great place just over here."

Well, boys will be boys, and men will be boys. There before us was a cliff face, which morphed downwards into a barren ravine. And behind us, there was no shortage of ammunition. We whooped as they bounced, thundered and spun. Some took giant leaps into space. Others exploded into pieces.

"Whoa! Did you see that one shatter on the bottom?" my nephew shouted. "Good one, Uncle Grant!"

"Well, wait till you see this one, John!" I called back. I grunted, lifted hard, and staggered toward the edge. My chosen super-boulder was heavy. It needed extra effort to launch it over the rim.

Immediately, I knew I had miscalculated. I tried to step back, but gravity was doing its work, sucking me over. I teetered. Without a doubt, I was going to follow that bouncing boulder to the bottom. Adrenaline pumped. Fear surged. Helpless. No way back. It's all over. I'm only thirty-five. Married eight years. Three small kids. And it's all over. My mouth opened to scream.

That's when an unseen hand grabbed my shirt.

I'll always be grateful that my climbing companion was right by my side. He could have been bringing up another boulder. He could have been three steps away, instead of the length of his young, strong arm.

FORTY-FOUR

THE PERVERT

MERMAID BEACH, QUEENSLAND, 2013

I've just finished my talk as guest speaker at the Mermaid Beach Rotary Club in Queensland. After question time, the meeting breaks up and I start signing books. I like to write a favourite Afghan proverb in each one, if I have time, such as "Dry riverbeds will once again overflow with water." I dare not pause once I start writing. If I look up, I can't see to return to my place, and it gets messy.

The guys start chatting and ordering another drink. "Can you direct me to the men's toilets," I ask Richard, my host.

"No problem, Grant. Go through the double doors and turn left."

"And …?"

"It's on your right. You can't miss it."

You mightn't miss it, Richard, but you're not vision impaired. I repeat the directions and he nods.

I sally forth through the double doors, turn left and, yes, down the wide hall there is another door to the right. A man in a black shirt is approaching from the other way. I'll check with him to make sure. You can't be too careful.

"Excuse me, is this the gentlemen's toilet?"

He looks my way but doesn't reply. I can't understand why he isn't answering. People are always ready to help someone with a white stick.

He lingers by the door, so I repeat the question. "Excuse me, sir. Is this the men's toilet?"

Again I wait for an answer, but there isn't one. He just stands there looking at me.

I wish I could actually see his face, but I have no focus these days. I'll give him the benefit of the doubt, though. Perhaps he is a newcomer to Australia and needs to learn more English. Or maybe he's a tourist from another country—they get a lot of them on the balmy Gold Coast when it's freezing on the northern side of the equator.

I push past him and through the door. Ah yes, a wide urinal comes into my fuzzy view. I'm in the right place.

The door swings open behind me. Two small boys chatter their way in. By the sound of the pressure against the wall and their speed of process, I am aware that their young bladders are much more elastic than mine. I'm envious. They have come and gone well before I can pull up my zip. With that silent guy wandering around, I'm glad there were two of them. There was something a bit creepy about him.

I push through the door and … oh, no! There he is. Black shirt and all. Who *is* this guy? Is he some kind of pervert? I'm not even going to speak to him this time. I turn on my heel and walk away. Perhaps Blackshirt notices my suspicion, because at the same time he turns and walks in the opposite direction.

I get back to the meeting room. I'm still a bit puzzled. Richard appears out of the fuzzy crowd.

"Welcome back!" He pauses, and I can feel his eyeballs analysing me. "Is everything OK, Grant?"

I take his elbow and we step aside. "Look, Richard, I'm a bit worried. A man is hanging around the door of the men's toilet."

Richard stiffens. "What? Who *is* he?"

"Could be some kind of pervert," I say. "He's wearing a black shirt. I asked him a couple of questions, but he wouldn't even answer me."

"I'll speak to the management right away. Can't be too careful these days. This is a family place, you know." He calls back over his shoulder, "Oh, your drink is on the table."

I look downwards and, more by feel than by sight, I find the glass. As I do so, something else looms into my peripheral vision. I start laughing—loudly.

"Come back, Richard," I shout.

All the blokes stop their chatting and drinking and stare at me.

Richard stops and turns.

"Please don't report him, Richard," I call out. "I can tell you who that pervert is."

"Who, Grant? Do you know the guy?"

"I know him well." I reach down and pull at my black shirt. "That guy is me. I've just worked out I was talking to a wall of mirrors across the end of the hall, right by the door of the men's toilets." I start laughing again.

All the men join in. Richard slaps my back. "Mirror, mirror on the wall," he shouts above the noise, "who is the blindest of them all?"

For a wise man,
a sign is sufficient.
AFGHAN PROVERB

Tom Cleary, Atoola Station, 2010.

FORTY-FIVE

MISCALCULATION 2

NORTHERN TERRITORY, 1983

A young voice comes from the backseat. "Dad, do you think we are going the right way?"
    Janna gives me a sideways glance. "That's what I've been wondering for the last hour."
    "No worries," I scoff. "Just look where the sun is."
    A sand goanna sprints across the bush track. I swerve a little, and wave my hand.
    "See! We're still heading north-east."
    I'm a bit miffed, and I hope they've picked it up in my tone. When you've spent as much time in the outdoors as I have, you get to know directions just by looking at which way the shadows fall. My Dad could tell the time, within minutes, by the position of the sun. Doesn't work on an overcast day, though, but hey! there's nothing but wide blue sky out here. They should have a bit more confidence in the driver.
    We cruise along in silence for another fifteen minutes.
    "We'll see the homestead anytime now," I say confidently.
    Seven-year-old Matt spots it first. "There it is, Dad!" He points past my shoulder. "Over there!"
    I smirk. "Aha! That'll be it alright."
    Janna leans forward, squints through the bloodwoods and the mulga, then catches her breath. "It looks a lot like the place we called into two hours ago."
    Angela pipes up from behind me. "It is! It's the same place, Dad! Same rusty roof. See, the sheds and cattle-yards are on the same side."
    My shoulders start to sag.
    Janna sends another arrow glance. "So much for the sun. We've just travelled in a great big circle. Probably one of their bore runs."
    My ego balloon has been shot to pieces.

"I wonder if anyone will be at home this time," Maria says, and puts her nose back into her book.

※

Every few years, I like to visit Central Australia. Not only does our family business sell top stud bulls to every state in Australia, as well as exporting them, but we also sell a lot of herd bulls to the cattle breeders in the outback.

"On this trip," I told Janna, "I want to take you and the kids. You haven't been up there for years, and they are all old enough now."

Janna smiled. She loves the wide open spaces. "Missing a bit of school won't hurt them," she said. "They'll learn lots."

So we sat down and planned the journey. We'd put the Volvo sedan on the train at Port Augusta. It would be fun for the family to do the rail trip to Alice Springs. We'd visit our client cattle stations in the Northern Territory and the top end of Western Australia, then drive back.

"It will be good to visit your sister," Janna says. "We haven't seen her for ages."

My sister Gaynor had been in the Territory for twenty years. She married a top stockman, Tom Cleary. Tom knew horses as well as cattle. As a young bloke, he'd spent months at a time in the saddle, droving big mobs of cattle across the Territory to the railhead in Queensland. He loved the way cattle responded to patient men on steady horses. But he could ride fast too. Whether it was out-flanking a breakaway mob, or jockeying for a win on the Alice Springs racetrack, he was a natural horseman. At the local Hartz Range annual picnic carnival, he was a legend. They even named a race after him. His ambition was to become a manager on one of the eastern stations. "No helicopters or motorbikes," was his philosophy. "Stir up the cattle too much. Give me horses every time," he'd grin. And Tom had a grin you could lose yourself in. My sister met him and his Akubra when she left our southern home to work on Mount Riddock Station, a thousand miles away.

At the time of our visit, they were working at Alcoota Station, about three hour's drive from Alice Springs. We would kill two birds with one stone. We'd spend family time with Gay and Tom, and I'd check out the cattle with Tom's boss, Tommy Webb, a regular buyer of our bulls. Then we'd drive on to Delny Station.

Gay and Tom gave us the directions. "It's just a bush track, and not much used," Tom said, "but you'll save a lot of time if you go up via Waite River Homestead. It's simple."

He grabbed a stick and drew a map in the dirt.

Janna looked at me. "Don't you think we should check it on the map, Grant?"

I tapped my forehead. "No need. I've got it all up here."

We said our goodbyes and headed off.

But as the old proverb says, "Pride comes before a fall."

※

Yes, the second time around there was someone at home at the rusty-roofed homestead. James was the manager, and he'd just pulled up at the shed in his one-ton truck. Two cattle dogs leapt off the back and proceeded to check the tyres of our Volvo sedan.

I introduced myself and told him the story.

He grinned. "Too bad I wasn't here. I was out on the eastern bore-run. Got held up on number 7. Had to replace the leathers in the windmill pump."

I nodded. I knew what he was talking about, and he would have had an empty water trough and a heap of thirsty cattle to greet him. Not good in this outback hot weather.

James leans forward and eyeballs me. "Were there any cattle hanging around the troughs on the western run?"

I'm still getting over feeling like a dummy, but I was glad to show I can be useful. "No, we passed four bores. The mills were all spinning and the troughs were full."

"See any of those fence-wrecking camels?" he drawls between tight lips. "Too many of those blasted humps around these days. Just go where they like."

I shook my head. James pushed his hat back off his forehead, "Well, you saved me a job. I won't have to check that run till tomorrow." He leads me to the end of the shed and points. "That's the track you should have taken, Grant. I'd have you in for a cuppa , but if you want to get there before dark, you'd better make tracks."

The kids disengage themselves from the tail-waggers and climb back into the car. The dogs yap after us for the first half mile, then head back through the dust to the homestead. We still have a long way to go.

FORTY-SIX

FUMES

NORTHERN TERRITORY, 1983

There is a lot of graffiti sprayed onto a big, steel water tank out in the middle of nowhere, way north east of Alice Springs. Numerous emblems of southern football teams overlap some rather unflattering remarks about politicians. Janna finds a permanent marker in the glove box of our Volvo and I stride toward the tank.

I'm trying not to show it, but I'm getting really worried. Haven't seen a soul or a vehicle since we left James and his dogs. That was over three hours ago. The fuel gauge, like the sun, is sinking lower and lower. I switched the air-conditioner off long ago, and things went pretty quiet in the back seat after I stopped and pulled out the spare petrol can. But, even with my most economical driving, the needle is well in the red.

Janna shares out the last box of raisins. Sure, we have spare water, but things are not good. And it's all my fault. My pig-headed miscalculations have burnt up the fuel we need now. Four tracks converge on this lonely water-tank. Which of the other three do we take?

Janna lifts her head from the map, and points, "I'm pretty sure it is that one."

Somehow the graffiti on the tank is kind of comforting, human beings have passed this way before. I look for a space between the sport and the politics. It might help to leave a message in case things go totally pear-shaped, and someone comes looking for us.

I start to write. "The Lock family is heading east. Nearly out of fuel." And I add the time and date. I felt embarrassed when I wrote it in front of my wife and three kids. Me, the outdoor man, the cattle breeder. Now we are about to run out of fuel in Australia's unforgiving outback. I get back into the car and take the eastern track. I'm gripping the wheel hard, expecting a splutter and cough at any moment.

Then Matt jabs a finger. "There's something, Dad!"

That little aboriginal community, with pepper trees around a small store, looked like heaven to me. And sitting on a box in the shade was a white-bearded Aboriginal man who looked to me like the angel Gabriel. And within ten feet of his shady spot was the most beautiful fuel bowser I had ever seen. The fumes of gurgling petrol smelt so good. It was the most expensive, and the cheapest, fuel I've ever purchased.

Our angel rocked the bowser handle back and forth. "You're on the right track," he said. "The station's not far away."

Well, before our long adventure was over, we had crossed the sandy Tanami Desert in our sedan, flown in cattle-mustering helicopters at Sturt Creek, and detoured around immovable bull buffaloes standing across the track to Numbulwar. We had swum in the hot springs at Mataranka and spotted crocodiles while cruising in Katherine Gorge.

I can never think about Central Australia without a little voice reminding me of my outback miscalculations. *You are a natural optimist, Grant. The glass is always half-full. But you allowed optimism to over-ride humility and wisdom. Don't waste that lesson.*

*

In 2010, after returning from Afghanistan, I visited the centre once again. Yes, Tom Cleary had fulfilled his dream. He proudly drove me around Atoola Station at the top end of the Simpson Desert, right in his mother's traditional Arunta country.

"Gaynor and I have been managing this place for twenty-one years now, and this is the best season we've ever had."

Even with my failing vision, I was amazed at the sea of green covering the red sand. Such growth seemed out of place, almost obscenely green. There were plains of grass and wildflowers, fat cattle and waterholes teeming with winged wildlife. We boiled the billy in the shade of a tree at Number 4 bore. Tom scanned the verdant plains and stiffened.

"There's a big Dingo out there!" He reached for his rifle, then lowered it. "Too far away … and that grass is far too tall." He turned to me and spoke quietly. "This growth will carry us into next year, but out here, Grant, you can never count on getting two seasons like this in a row." He took a stick and lifted the boiling billy off the coals. "That's the biggest miscalculation you can make."

FORTY-SEVEN

WELCOMELY OBSCENE

ATOOLA STATION, 2010

Endless land, of grass-covered sand:
Woolly oat and buffel
Kerosene and button
The sand that made the centre red
Is hidden by a bed of paper daisy,
Perfumed by native stock,
Prodigious plumes of spinifex,
And golden corkwood blooms.

Last year this was the dusty grave
Of un-trucked cows,
And ghostly calves too weak to draft,
While haughty camels browsed,
And laughed through elevated jaws.

But now, *all* of nature laughs,
Intoxicated by the clouds of rain,
And forgetting desiccating years of pain,
Heartily guffaws.

On the Sandover and Plenty,
Pelicans and swans
Sweep long o'er seldom-seen lagoons.
Twenty thousand wood ducks can't be wrong,
Their whistling wings join finches' party tunes,
And the psychedelic throngs of busy budgerigars.

After browned out years,
Parched despair,
Grit-grinding debt,
And dust-choked air,
The post-drought growth seems obscenely green.
Welcomely obscene,
Emerald reality of a phantom dream.

No red between the mulga, bloodwood and
    ghost-white gum …
But it will return,
It will come,
As sure as stormy summer fires will scorch
    and burn the run.

But we're so thankful for the rains which soak,
And fill the dusty plains with two seasons at least,
Of laughter and hope,
For man and beast.

※

Postscript. Two years later, like many surrounding cattle stations, over half of Atoola was burnt out by bushfires started by rainless electrical storms.

FORTY-EIGHT

FLASHMAN

KABUL, 2004

You'd have to be impressed by Brigadier-General Sir Harry Paget Flashman, VC, KCB, KCIE, in his dashing Hussars cavalry uniform. A Victoria Cross and a knighthood, both direct from the hand of Queen Victoria herself. He saw action in the Charge of the Light Brigade, the Indian Mutiny and almost every other major British war of the mid to late nineteenth century. Skilled in foreign languages and horsemanship, master of espionage and escapes, he deserved Her Majesty's recognition.

By his own written admission, Flashman carried a selfish streak, but don't we all? He also confessed that he was a compulsive womaniser and that he struggled with cowardice. But it's clear from his diaries that he was brave and inventive when cornered. His actions turned the tide of a number of British campaigns.

Late in life, Harry Flashman wrote his memoirs, wrapped them in oilskin covers and placed them in a tea-chest. There they remained, untouched, for fifty years, until they were auctioned off with household furniture and fell into the hands of a journalist with the *Glasgow Times*, George Macdonald Fraser. He quit his job and edited and published them campaign by campaign. The first volume appeared in 1969 and was Flashman's personal account of his involvement in the first Anglo-Afghan War. He was one of only two British men who survived the bloodbath.

I was sucked in from the beginning.

Back in January 1842, an exhausted horse carried its wounded mount to the garrison outpost at Jalalabad, staggered to the stable floor and never rose again. It is commonly held that Assistant Surgeon Dr William Brydon was the only British man to survive the wrath of the Afghans. But Harry Flashman fought his way out too. And we would never have known that if it hadn't been for those unread papers found by Macdonald Fraser.

At that time, the British, under ambitious Sir William Macnaghten, thought they had control of Afghanistan. But governing Afghanistan was, as they say these days, like herding cats. The cats were very well behaved for a while. Then, when the British had been lulled into complacency, Sir William Macnaghten was invited to a picnic.

Macnaghten was blind—blinded not by retinal failure, like me—but by his own self-importance. He was blinded by his visions of climbing another velvet rung on the ladder of the British Raj. Was he not the one who knew best how to handle these uncivilised Afghan princes? And wasn't his the hand that moved the lips of Shah Shujah, the puppet king, thus keeping the Russian bear from sinking its claws into British India?

Yes, all was going well for Macnaghten. Sure, there were some rumblings out there, but that was normal enough. Nothing he couldn't handle. He had four-and-a-half thousand troops to back him up. And they were well supported by twelve thousand camp followers, from officer's wives, farriers and gunsmiths to herdsmen, valets and washer women.

But Macnaghten was totally sucked in. In between the cricket matches, Madeira wine, garden parties and cigars, Sir William should have studied a few of the local proverbs:

"The only time the Pashtuns stop fighting is when they go to war."

"I got my revenge, and I did it quickly. It took a hundred years."

Yes, Afghans know how to wait, and how to choose the right moment. Like the winter picnic, out on the snowy fields of Kabul, well away from the Bala Hissar, the Great Fort, which had been captured by the British. But Macnaghten and his army's leadership had become sloppy. After all, the Bala Hissar was a long way up the mountain. Janna and I have hiked up there and it's quite a haul. Much better to garrison on the plains. Closer to the fabled Kabul bazaars, exotic food, eastern entertainment and veiled women.

It all happened so quickly. The picnic knives, plus a few longer ones, came out. Sir William's body was paraded around town, in six separate pieces. It was the beginning of the end for Britain's Army of the Indus.

Over sixteen thousand souls were butchered, either in Kabul or on the flight back to India through the mountain passes. Those whom the swords and the long-barrelled *jezails* did not exterminate, the deep snow consumed. It was a debacle, the greatest humiliation ever suffered by the British Empire until Singapore fell to bicycles, bayonets and Japanese jungle boots exactly one hundred years later.

There are times in our lives when what we hold dear proves to be a lie. The myth that the most powerful empire of its day could subjugate Afghanistan was one of those phantoms. In more recent times, that same mirage drove the Soviet invasion of Afghanistan on Christmas Day 1979. But herding cats is tough work, dangerous work, costly work. That's why, ten years later, the Russians were compelled to leave the "Graveyard of Empires". It is well argued that the blood, bullets and bullion expended in those Afghan mountains were responsible for the collapse of the Soviet Union.

Colonel Beg of the Pakistan Intelligence Service summed it up in a different way. "For a foreign power to control Afghanistan, and bring unity and success, it is like the shopkeeper in the bazaar, weighing frogs on his hand-held scales. When one jumps off, he retrieves it, but while he is replacing it, another leaps off."

And now, as the Americans and NATO pull out and Afghanistan goes it alone, may the country somehow grow in a unity which allows development that benefits the big and the small. We cling to the sentiment of another old Afghan proverb: "The world lives in hope."

Well, I can't point the finger, because I was completely sucked in by Harry Flashman. It was a lie that he struggled through the blood-stained snow to escape the wrath of the Afghans. I was totally blinded by Macdonald Fraser's fictitious hero, and by his cleverly footnoted Flashman books. Those footnotes included many verifiable facts of history. I checked them out. It was all so convincing!

I had the whole collection of eleven volumes. Found them in second-hand bookshops in Islamabad, where diplomatic types with deeper pockets than ours jettisoned their libraries prior to moving on. We loved those little cluttered bookshops with their musty, well-read smells. You could dig through the delightfully claustrophobic aisles and walk out with everything from *The Great Game* to books on Turkish carpets,

American presidents and Eastern art, plus copies of Agatha Christie and Macdonald Fraser's next revelation of my hero, Harry Flashman.

Yes, I was totally sucked in. Did I not visit Flashman's Hotel on Mall Road, Rawalpindi? It was built in his honour on the very route he used as he traversed the British Raj in the service of Queen Victoria. I sat in it. I ate tasty buffalo steaks in it. And I studied his portrait in it.

Was there a British Raj? True.

Was there a siege at Khartoum? True.

Was there a Taiping Rebellion? True.

Did Brigadier-General Sir Harry Flashman faithfully serve Queen Victoria in each of these places? False.

Harry Flashman never existed.

I felt so stupid when I discovered the lie. I went red in the face as I thought of how I had raved about Flashman to friends and family. Yet I secretly admire the late Macdonald Fraser for his ability to write so convincingly.

It's comforting to know I wasn't the only one. Apparently the novels deceived many US academic critics as well.

I had been sucked in by one of the truly great storytellers.

FORTY-NINE

THE RIFLE

THE BUSH, 2009

When he used it yesterday, fifty-three corpses slumped to the ground.
 This time, he'll have to be extra careful. Make a mistake, and he'll be locked in the body of a paraplegic. And that's not the plan.

※

"Sorry, Joe," the amiable stock agent said as he climbed out of the dusty sheep-yard. "You'll have to deal with the ones I've marked; they're too weak to make the trip. But the rest should sell to the re-stockers. The truck will be here tomorrow morning, early, and the cheque will be in your hands by the end of the week."
 Joe looks away and says nothing. *Yeah, what cheque? By the time they take out the selling fees, the transport and the tax, it won't be much of a cheque!*
 The agent knows what Joe is thinking. But what can he do, except lay a dust trail to the next hurting farm?
 Joe reaches for the rifle and checks the magazine. *Top ewes, too! Worn themselves down with another lamb. Gave it their all, and what do they get? A bullet in the forehead, and then a mass burial.*
 He slowly moves through the thinning mob. Shot follows shot. Drop follows drop. The bodies quiver, then lay still. It gets harder and harder.

The pungent smell of blood-soaked sheep-yard dust rises to his nostrils.

Should have got the neighbour to come and do it. Those big eyes look up at you ... and then you pull the trigger. It's like shooting your children. You're no good, Joe. You're a failure.

Back in the farm workshop, he sits and stares at the oil stains on the concrete floor, and feels the comforting weight of the wood and metal in his hands. "I should be in that hole with them," he says quietly.

"You're right, Joe. That's where you should be," the voice whispers. "Just do it. One squeeze and it's all over. It's the only way."

He reaches for a cloth. *Bad luck, escape, a raw deal ... what does it matter? One squeeze of the finger and it's done. The loneliness, the if onlys and that voice will all be gone.*

He folds the cloth and rubs hard on the end of the barrel. *You can get the bloodstains off, but you can't stop that whispering voice.* "Face up to it, Joe. You're no good. The season's had it—and so have you."

Outside the shed, dust swirls as another droughty change blows through. A loose sheet of iron flaps on the empty hay-shed roof.

Flap, flap, flap.

Flap, flap, flap.

You're, no, good.

You're, no, good.

Joe's jaw tightens and he scowls at the oil-stained floor.

So much for Old Charlie. "Yeah," he said, pulling his great hairy ear. "I reckon this cold front will be a good one. Coming in from the north-west too. Full moon and all. It'll rain for sure!" But Old Charlie is still pulling his ear, and we've had two full moons since then. You can't keep buying hay. Not when the bank manager is watching every transaction. The cash has been flowing but all the wrong way!

Joe scans the workshop. The grinder, the drill press, the welder. It's his favourite place. The tools hang on the shadow-board. Every spare part is in its place. There's nothing to fix because nothing is broken. Nothing is broken because nothing is being used. Nothing is being used because there is no rain.

Good thing Marj has the librarian's job at the local school. She'll be OK. Better off without me. It hasn't been fair on her. After she pays for the groceries, the rest just goes to hold back the tsunami of accruing interest. Then on the weekends, she's helping me move stock from one barren paddock to another, or taking a turn on the tractor.

I've let her down. Would have been better if we'd never met at that country ball when she first came out here. But I couldn't take my eyes off her. We talked and talked. She planned to travel, see the world. "A couple of good seasons," I stupidly promised, "and we'll do it together." I can still feel the squeeze of her hand, and the press of her firm body as we swayed through the modern waltz. That was twenty-five years ago. Now the only travel she does is that twenty kilometres of bone-rattling road between the farm and the school. We stopped talking long ago.

I've failed her. I see it in her eyes—when I have the guts to look into them.

And the kids—they both left. Jill hated moving to the city, but that's where the work is. She always looked so good in the saddle. She's gone, and so have the horses, and now most of the sheep. She longs to be back on the farm and, wouldn't you know it, her mother longs to be back in the city.

And we don't hear anything from young Clive these days. Took off for the big money at the mines. Can't blame him. "There's no future here, Dad," he kept saying. "You can't stop global warming." He was the smart one. From that good season three years ago, he got paid out with his pride and joy: the V8 Holden ute. And after the next gut-wrenching, rainless winter, he put his foot on the throttle and roared off to Western Australia.

How much can a man take? How long can you hold up the mask? How many times can you say, "Yeah, I'm OK," when it's just the anti-depressants talking? And there are always the whispers, cycling through your head.

The TV hasn't helped. You flip from the same depressing weather forecast to *The X Factor* or *Master Chef*. They're the lucky ones. Their uncertainty only lasts a few minutes. You can see their eyes voicelessly pleading, "Pick me! I want to get into the next round. Pick me!"

Well, I won't be here for the next round. I've had enough. The rock in my belly is too heavy. The hope in my soul has long dried up, like the few piddly showers we've had this year. And the financial review is due tomorrow.

I know what it will be like. Put on a clean pair of jeans. Have the guy with the tie survey me across his nice polished desk and spell it out. "You have to realise, Joseph," he'll say, "the bank has its shareholders to look after." Well, I won't be there to hear it. I won't be there to feel the squeeze of his precious shareholders and their humiliating straight jacket. The farm's worth almost nothing now. The neighbours *aren't interested. They've got their own reviews to get through.*

I'm a failure. Why should she put up with me any longer?

In the States, they say, you can buy a handgun across the counter. Well, it would be a damn sight easier to slide a pistol into my mouth than this clumsy rifle. I need to do this right. I don't want to be trapped here as a vegetable.

There's a distant throaty roar. It gets louder. That rumbling V8 sounds familiar. Rusty runs yapping to meet it.

All the way across the Nullarbor, Clive has been practising his lines.

Yeah, Mum rang. Said it's been rough without rain. But I've quit the mining now. Really missed the footy matches and dances, and the beers with the guys. Done well, though, Dad. One thing about those outback drilling rigs—the pay is good, and you don't get to spend much money. So I'm back. I reckon I'll take my chances on the farm. It can't stay dry forever.

He leans his weight against the wide doors of the workshop, and they slowly rumble open. "Hey, Dad, I'm back!"

But the cashed-up prodigal is one kilometre, one dry month, one last squeeze too late.

A week after the funeral, the season changes. Clive gets the crop planted and there's enough moisture underneath to take it through to a good harvest. The remaining sheep are putting on weight, and the bank manager is smiling.

The hardest part is pushing open those rumbling workshop doors. And over in the corner steel cabinet, with its magazine full, minus one, is the rifle with its bloodstained barrel.

For two years now, Clive has tried to ignore that cabinet. But he's had enough. He strides to the far corner, throws open the door, draws back, turns and looks around the workshop. He spies the leather welding gloves, grunts and returns to the cabinet. With protected hands, he carries the contaminated weapon to the bench and lays it beneath the hydraulic press. There is a scraping sound as the press forces the barrel into a right angle. Clive releases the machine and, with both arms hurls the metal boomerang through the doors and onto the scrap heap. It clatters, quivers, then lies still.

He pulls off the gloves, rolls the doors shut and strides to the ute. He gives half a wave to the weeping woman on the homestead veranda and guns the throttle.

Two hundred metres down the track, the brake lights shine through the lifting dust. Marj holds her breath. There is a low whistle. Rusty leaps in and settles between the hard hat and the driver.

The V8 roars.

Marj buries her face in her hands and inhales deeply.

No one hears her scream.

FIFTY
AND THE WINNER IS...

ADELAIDE, NOVEMBER 2013

"Sorry," says Wade, "all the $2 sweeps have been taken. And the $5 ones as well."

I grimace. I did want to have my annual flutter on the Race that Stops the Nation.

He smiles, "But there are still two places left in the $10 sweep."

I wave a note in the air. "That's not much help, mate. I only have $5 with me."

Now Wade's a good bloke—does a great job running the gym. He's cheerful, positive and encouraging. So it's no surprise when he says, "Tell you what, Grant. I haven't had a shot yet. I'll throw in the other $5 and you can pick the horse."

"Ok," I say, and I pull out one of the last two folded pieces of paper. "You hang on to it, Wade." He knows I can no longer read.

Having ticked that little box in today's mental to-do list, I head for the bench press. I don't know what it is about the bench press, but I always start my workout that way.

With my brain cleared by a good session, I head for home and get stuck into another chapter of my book.

✺

Time flies when I'm writing. The clock gremlins wait till I am absorbed, then they put the hands into over-drive.

The phone rings. It's Wade. "Did you watch the race, Grant?"

I check the clock. "Oh no! I missed it! How did we go?"

"Are you ready for the good news?"

"Absolutely!" My mind is already doing the maths. *Twenty-four horses at ten dollars. Half for me and half for Wade. Awesome!*

"Congratulations, Grant. You picked the winner of the Melbourne Cup."

"Wowee! Fantastic!" I start jumping round, waving my mobile.

Wade is trying to say something. I return the phone to my ear. "Yes?"

"But there is some not-so-good news, Grant."

A cloud is forming on the horizon. "Like what, Wade?"

※

Actually, I'm not big into horse racing. But who could fail to be stirred by gutsy gallopers like our incredible Phar Lap? Or Seabiscuit, who raised the morale of millions of Americans during the Great Depression? There is something about a racehorse straining for the winning post, pulling away from its competitors or surging from behind to reach the line. And what about our fantastic Aussie phenomenon, Black Caviar? Twenty-five races and twenty-five wins, including that heart-stopping finish at Royal Ascot.

Then there are some great horses of history that stir me. Bucephalus, Alexander the Great's wonderful stallion, died near Jhelum in what is modern-day Pakistan, where I worked for twenty years. And think of Banjo Patterson's wiry mountain horse in *The Man from Snowy River*:

> The wild hop scrub grew thickly,
>   and the hidden ground was full
> Of wombat holes, and any slip was death.
> But the man from Snowy River let the pony have his head,
> And he swung his stockwhip round and gave a cheer,
> And he raced him down the mountain
>   like a torrent down its bed,
> While the others stood and watched in very fear.

And what about Lady Godiva's famous ride, and the temptation to lay eyes on the bare-skinned benefactor? It was all too much for Tom; he couldn't drill that hole in the shutters fast enough.

Then there were the tough Mongolian mounts of Genghis Khan's cavalry. The blitzkrieg of the thirteenth century, they gave their leader the largest empire the world had ever seen.

And talking of cavalry, my emotions move into top gear when I consider the charge of the 4th Light Horse Brigade. If you have one drop of Aussie or Kiwi blood in you, you could not fail to be stirred by the last great cavalry charge in history. Every Anzac Day, I like to reread the account of the charge on Beersheba with its life-giving wells, stuck away in the Palestinian desert. Instead of dismounting and taking cover on foot, those young blokes from the city and the bush obeyed the order to charge their parched mounts straight into Turkish machine gun fire. The Turks could not adjust their weapons fast enough.

Why don't we hear more about these Light Horsemen who did what their brave mates had been unable to do two years earlier at Gallipoli?

Then there was Spear, the horse that saved my grandfather up in the Flinders Ranges. Lost in a two-day dust storm, Grandpa Steve followed the birds. His desiccated mount carried him to water. Ironically, it was the hooves of his bolting horse-team that sent the great stockman to a premature grave.

And I recall the two-wheeled, horse-drawn *tongas* where we worked in Pakistan. On one of my wife's trips into town, her Pakistani lady companions were unusually friendly. Too friendly. When she reached the bazaar, Janna could not find her purse.

When I think about it, there are a lot of horses in my life. In my imagination—and in that vision.

Yes, I had a vision once. It happened in Peshawar, Pakistan—the very city where, many years later, a church where we worshipped was torn apart by Islamic terrorists, killing over one hundred, and where later still, the brave Taliban, the fighters of God, systematically gunned down defenceless school students, with an even greater death toll.

No, it wasn't a dream. Dreams often fade, but you always remember a vision—it sticks in your mind.

I was standing listening to a great sound. A rider on a white horse galloped toward me. There was something powerful, desirable and beautiful about him. It was clear he wasn't stopping. He was on a mission. His face blazed with joy and destiny. I wanted to be part of what he was doing. It seemed good, right and exciting. But I knew there was no way I could join him. Then, as the rider thundered past, he leaned over, grabbed me and swung me up behind him. It was so exhilarating to be wanted, to be included. The joy, the purpose, the reality and the meaning all came together. The rider was powerful and radiant. He looked to me like a man. Yet when I looked again, it was a lamb, living yet as if slaughtered.

I have never forgotten it, even though it happened twenty-five years ago.

※

Wade is still on the phone, and I am waiting for his not-so-good news. "Come on, Wade! Have we won or haven't we?"

"Well, Grant, you definitely picked the winner of the Melbourne Cup." He pauses, like they do on *The X-Factor*. "It's just that, timing-wise, you made a bad choice."

Do I detect a smirk? "Bad choice?"

"Yes. Our horse, Green Moon, won the Cup all right. But that was last year. This year, he came fourth last!" My shoulders slump. "Hey, Grant, we were only out by twelve months! Perhaps we'll have better luck next time. Cheers!"

Well, we missed out. But our venture has caused me to mull over some great horses, and some great rides. And there are many more. But surely the greatest ride of all was one taken by that rider who joyfully hoisted me up to join him. It all happened just ninety kilometres north of Beersheba.

> Innocent man.
> Kangaroo court.
> Politics, power, position.
> Hatred, anger, money.
> He defied them all,
> riding into the jaws of death
> not on a Ben-Hur chariot,
> not on a Macedonian warhorse,
> but on a donkey.

FIFTY-ONE

THE TOUCH

ADELAIDE, 2014

Heart-beat of the universe
Revealer of secrets
give breath.
Fill the vacuum
of this inverted soul
screaming
for meaning
gripping the reins of death
galloping the stallion of rebellion
into
independent
loneliness.

Then
He reached out
and He touched me
and
with outstretched hands
oozing the blood of love
He embraced me,
sparked the flames
stained my soul.
And though he left
He still remains.

A broken hand can work,
but a broken heart cannot.
AFGHAN PROVERB

FIFTY-TWO

THE SQUATTERS

ADELAIDE, 2013

Just when we thought the Eastern suburbs of Adelaide were a quiet place to settle, someone torched a car in our street. And then the squatters arrived.

They carried personal weapons and were well organised. At 2.15 pm, in broad daylight, they took over the small house next to our Magill home.

Janna heard them coming. In no time, they were through the front entrance and inside.

"It's not right!" She peers through the window. "They can't just take over a place like that, even if it is empty. Can't you do something, Grant?"

I've always been slower than my irrepressible wife in weighing things up. I am upset, but she is fuming. But what can I do? We're outnumbered, and I can see they have guards out the front. We could get hurt.

"I wish it hadn't been left empty for so long," I say.

Yes, our nearest neighbours left at the start of summer, and we don't expect them back till August.

Janna is deeply offended by the blatant intrusion and she is not giving up. "You have to do something, Grant. It looks like they plan to stay."

I join her at the window. "Well, what do you suggest? I can't go out there—there's too many of them."

"Can't you call someone?"

"But, Janna, the police wouldn't come. I know exactly what they would say. 'Sorry, sir, we can't get involved yet. We suggest you ring the council first.'"

"In that case, why don't you pick up the phone?"

I finally get through. A sweet-voiced young woman interrogates me. "Is the house on Campbelltown City Council land?"

"Well, no, but—"

"Sorry, sir, if it's a private home, we can't get involved."

"We can't get involved." I parrot the words in my mind. That's the mantra of our inward-looking, individualistic society. The widow gets mugged in public. The girl gets mauled on the bus. But nothing happens because we don't want to get involved. "Do unto others" becomes "Don't do anything."

The council woman is still on the phone. "We're really sorry, sir. However, there is one thing we can do. We can provide the name of someone who will come and evict them—for a fee, of course."

Janna is still peering through the window, like a jumpy meerkat on caffeine overload.

"Look," I say to Ms Sweetlips, "I don't live in the house. I just want to do something so it's empty when the neighbours come back. If it involves money, I know they don't have any."

"Hold on, sir, there's another number here. Apparently this man will do it for free. Seems he does it for a hobby."

He evicts unwanted tenants for a hobby? And for free? I'm not sure I want to meet this tough guy. Not sure about his values or his methods.

I take down the number, but I've already decided what I'm going to do for our absentee neighbours. I have become fond of them and their kids, despite the fact they use a language I don't understand. It's a singsong sort of dialect—nothing like the Urdu we spoke in Pakistan, or the Dari we learnt in Afghanistan.

We are mostly traditional European Australians in this part of suburbia, and these guys have brought some colour and interest to the street. Yes, we all need a bit of structure, but too much of the familiar and commonplace can drown you in the swamp of urban ordinariness. That all went out of the window when the noisy neighbours came last September. We made them welcome and offered them a drink, which they appreciated. We could have helped them shift in, but they are an independent lot and like to do things their own way.

We first saw them when they were checking the place out. It's timber framed, small and a bit draughty, but they seemed happy with it. Then, about the time I thought they were really settled, they and their kids suddenly up and left. Sad, really—we were just getting to know them.

Some other locals, who seem to know more about them than we do, said they'd be back before August, so we keep looking out for them. But now we have this unexpected invasion by a bunch that looks like being very unpleasant neighbours. I have an idea, though: I'll get them moving before they get too comfortable.

Janna notices the fresh resolve on my face. She follows me to the shed. "What are you going to do, Grant?

I might be slow at getting mobilised, but once I get motivated, I get motivated. "I'm going to make a bomb. We have to show them they're not wanted around here."

Behind her new rimless glasses, her brown eyes are like saucers. "No, Grant! Please! Not a bomb!"

I guess it's because of our four years in Afghanistan. You never knew where a bomb would go off next. The Taliban are very clever at that sort of thing. And back in Pakistan, they bombed the church when everyone was praying. Some of our friends lost their lives, others their hearing.

"No, no! It's not a real bomb." I fossick through the rag and fertiliser cupboard. "It's just a smoke bomb. I'll set it up tonight when they're sleeping."

Her jaw returns to a more normal position. "You'd better watch out or you'll set the place on fire."

"Well, they might think it's the best of times, free housing and all," I smirk, "but when they get a whiff of *this,* it'll be the worst of times." I reach for the kerosene. "Do you have any cooking oil? That'll make lots of smelly smoke."

"Yes, but—!"

"Hey! Stop worrying! I'll fix it so that it won't start a fire."

"Look, Grant, I don't like that nasty bunch any more than you do. Go ahead and smoke them out. But if the place is full of soot and smoky smells, will it ever be habitable again?"

"I hope so! I just love the cheerful chatter of those eastern rosellas." I scratch around for a box of matches. "But one thing is absolutely sure: there's no way they'll come back to our birdhouse if those confounded bees become permanent residents!"

Well, I evicted those bees from the birdhouse all right. But they were soon back.

FIFTY-THREE

WHEN THE PLANETS ALIGN

ADELAIDE, 2013

Planet 1. Janna Lock
Passionate about serving widows back in Kabul. She listened to them, drank tea with them, mentored them and empowered them by finding markets for their embroidery.

Planet 2. Roy the bee man
Turns out I know this tall guy from our farming and cattle breeding days on the Eyre Peninsula. He takes away the birdhouse, squatter-bees and all. Invites us to speak at Stirling.

Planet 3. The ravenous readers
A reading club. They have just read my book *Shoot Me First* and are keen to support Janna's project. They turn up at the meeting ready to give.

Planet 4. A group of Afghan widows and their kids
The government has parked them out in a stony valley. They walk for miles to get water. If only they had a well!

Planet 5. Barbara
Our colleague back in Afghanistan. She knows the widows well and receives the funds Janna sends.

Planet 6. The royal squatter
The Queen Bee who won't leave her new home.

Now the planets have all aligned.

Janna is reading an email from Barbara.

> Dear Janna,
>
> Please thank the generous folks for sending the money. The extra came just in time. You know Bibi Rasool. Well, she and ten other families, mainly widows, have had to move to a remote and barren valley. There was no other place for them to go. They have to walk two miles to get water. It has been really tough for them. Last winter was extra snowy, and they ran out of the thorn bushes they had collected for fuel.
>
> We managed to find some funds for Bibi Rasool to start digging a well. Her diggers got down to twenty-four metres and struck a huge rock. They were going to quit. The money had run out. But your timely funds kept them going. And the miracle is that after they broke up the stone, they found water. Good water! And you know what plenty of water means: hygiene, less disease, less medicine, fewer deaths and a small vegetable garden. They can put their energy into using clay and water to make sundried bricks and extend their simple homes. Some of them have ten people living in one room.
>
> Apart from Bibi Rasool we have just found Zamina here in Kabul. She is about twenty-five but looks fifty-five. Her four stunted children look like dwarfs. Her husband left to find work four years ago and never came back. She found work in the bazaar cracking almonds. The shopkeeper never pays her cash. Her pay is the almond shells. She uses some for fuel and trades some for bread.
>
> Thank you very much for helping care for the Bibi Rasools and Zaminas of Afghanistan.
>
> Barbara

Janna lays down the printout she has been reading aloud and stares silently beyond me. She is back in Kabul, sitting with the women she loves.

Finally she looks at me and smiles. "That's wonderful. And those women will never know that they owe their water to a bunch of Aussie bees and their stubborn Queen."

Give by the pound,
take by the ounce.
AFGHAN PROVERB

FIFTY-FOUR

HEALING

ADELAIDE 2013

These events are true. Some names have been changed to protect the innocent—and the guilty.

※

I went to a healing meeting yesterday. My eyes need healing. And I know God is going to do it. Just not sure which side of heaven he plans for it to happen.

But I wasn't in a very good frame of mind because there's something else I need fixed: a slow internet connection.

Months before I had signed up with Belstra. A high-speed cable runs past our house. Countless Belstra door knockers had reminded me of that. But in the end it was the Belstra shop that got my business. I'm not stupid. If I want to sign up for that fast cable, I need a physical location to go back to, "just in case." I was soon to learn that, with Belstra, "just in case" was to be almost every case.

"Yes, sir," the young salesman said, "just sign here and you'll be all connected in five to ten days."

Great. I couldn't wait.

※

Now the preacher in the meeting is sharing. "It's a matter of trust," he says. "The good Word declares that God confounds the world's wisdom. He is almighty. He is the healer."

I know all that stuff, and I believe it. Sure, God doesn't always work to *our* time frames. But I've been through enough with him to know that I can trust him.

The preacher's mouth is still moving, but I'm only half listening. I'm thinking about the giant mess-up Belstra has made. It all started well, but now it's incongruous even to mention 'Belstra' and 'trust' in the same sentence.

※

The door chime rings. It's a young bloke with a logo on his shirt. "Hi, I'm from Belstra. I'm here to get you connected. Before I leave, you'll be running on high speed cable internet!"

"That's good." I show him in. "At last, we'll have reliable Skype connections and uninterrupted video chats with our grandkids in Singapore, Canada and Melbourne."

"Not a problem," young Mr Confident Belstra says. "Just show me the room where the cable connection comes in."

I stare at him. "But … it doesn't come in!"

He stares back.

I raise my palms. "It's not into the house yet. I told them that when I signed up!"

His shoulders sag a little, but not much. "Sorry," he says, "I only do the inside stuff. I don't do cable connections."

I stand there half-stunned. It's like when they call out your number at a raffle and you can't find your ticket.

He hands me a card. "Just ring this number."

I want to say, "Hold on mate! It's not my fault. Why can't *you* ring the number?" But he is gone.

I ring Belstra. After I explain my problem, I am cheerfully rotated from one department to another.

"Hold on, sir, while I transfer you."

Nice music.

"Please hold—your call is important to us."

More music.

"I'm transferring you now."

You get to know the music so well, your brain is humming the tune next day.

"We apologise for the delay. Please hold."

I feel like a forgotten suitcase on the airport carousel.

Finally, someone in Belstraland lifts me off the conveyor belt. For the third time I explain my problem.

"The best thing to do," says the pleasant girl in Asian English, "is to re-book it. Mmm, let me check. Ah yes, we can do that on the 18th."

"That's good, that's only three days away."

"Oh no, sir! Not this month. Next month!"

I pause. "Did you say *next* month?"

"Yes, sir. That's the very first opportunity."

I hear myself give an insipid "OK".

My brain says, *Why did you say that, you big wimp! It's not "OK"! Give her a piece of your mind! You're a rational human being, aren't you? Ask her the obvious question: "Why not now?"*

But I can't. I've had the Belstra preconditioning treatment. It's all those countless departments. Your brain feels like an inert billiard ball ricocheting off a never-ending succession of cushions.

It's all been designed by some communications psychologist, just to wear you down. They know that, like Pavlov's dogs, you'll go half crazy, and you'll sink to your knees and give in—just a blob of jelly whispering into a telephone.

Then she says in a most congenial tone, "Now, sir, is there anything else I can do for you?"

I ought to scream, "OF COURSE there is something you could do for me! What a STUPID question! What about GETTING US CONNECTED?" Instead, I give a weak "No" and hang up. I hate myself for it. And so, I suspect, does my wife.

❉

The healer is speaking quietly. He is not shouting at God to do this or that. He looks around our friends' lounge room.

"Is there anyone else here who wants prayer? Who trusts in God?"

Well, I certainly trust in God, and I am always up for a blessing. I rise. "It's my eyes. I've got a genetic form of macular degeneration. They say it's incurable."

He moves forward, places his hands over my eyes and prays, then moves on. I immediately see a new brightness. Or is it just because my eyes were covered for a while?

❉

The door chime rings. "I'm from Belstra," the tall technician says. "I've come to connect your cable."

My jaw drops. "But just two days ago they said it would be next month, on the 18th!"

He waves a sheet of paper. "Here's the order. I can come back if you like."

I grab his shoulder. "No, no! Come in."

How good is this! They're going out of their way to correct their mistake. All is well.

The technician gets to work and I go to the kitchen. "Hey Janna, he says we'll have the high speed internet going in no time."

My wife purses her lips and continues to stir her raspberry muffin mix. "That's what the last one said."

I hold back my thoughts. *Unbeliever! Doesn't she know that this is our day? Our moment? It is all coming together.*

And just to prove my point, within ninety minutes Mr Trusty Belstra is sitting at my computer adjusting the settings. "See, it's all registered. Belstra will activate automatically within one hour." At the door he pauses. "Thanks for the coffee. Just ring this number if something goes wrong. But it won't!"

But it does!

✴

The healer has quietly moved to the wheelchair. These days she can only move her head and talk quietly. She's in the prison of multiple sclerosis. A recent poll says the disability that people dread most is blindness. Well, I'm legally blind and the middle of my vision is an opaque blob, but there is no way I would trade my fuzzy eyes for that restrictive wheelchair. I'd rather be blind.

He's talking about trust again. "You can trust God—he is able to heal." I really believe that. Hasn't he made our bodies with wonderful, everyday capacities? The cut, the break, the worn-out cells? And, yes, he can heal in dramatic ways too.

When the preacher prays over that wheelchair, I can say "Amen". That's because of our colleague back in Pakistan. Dr Molly Pont's multiple sclerosis got worse and worse. She was a surgeon in a remote hospital near the Afghan border, and depended on her electric scooter to take her to the operating theatre. There was prayer, and slowly she returned to belting that bird around on the badminton court.

And as for me, hey! I've already had one miracle. Most people with my eye disease lose their central vision before they are twenty. I've had forty-five wonderful bonus years on top of that.

※

After another phone ride on the Belstra merry-go-round, I finally make connection with the activation team. "The cable is connected. Could you activate us please?"

Pause.

"You are connected?"

"Yes. The technician came today."

Long pause.

"But why did the technician come today?"

I'm wondering what is going on. *Why wouldn't he come today? Isn't that how Belstra makes money? They hook people up and charge them for it.*

I stay positive and smile down the phone, "Well, all you have to do now is to activate us."

"But, sir, that's not possible."

"Not possible?"

"Not today. It's scheduled for the 18th of next month."

"But *your* technician said it's all ready to go!"

"Sorry, sir. It will be done on the 18th."

"Hold on! That's five weeks away!"

But nothing logical or illogical will move her. It is clear that some dates cannot be changed, like Christmas Day and my internet activation date.

Then comes that ubiquitous phone finale. "Grant, is there anything else I can do for you?" I moan and hang up, and my brain says, "Wimp."

Deep in the silicon jungle of Belstra's computers there is a little key to be pressed. That key is pressed, not to ignite the rockets of a space shuttle, not to focus a maze of radio telescopes on a distant new planet, not to launch a high-speed Japanese train, but simply to switch on my internet. How hard is that?

Janna appears with a stiff cup of coffee. "You have to say," she smirks, "Belstra is a great communications company."

I shovel in extra sugar and growl, "How is that?"

"Well, they really look after our security."

I raise an eyebrow.

"It's true! They never communicate anything between their own departments, let alone to anyone else. Our personal details are always perfectly safe."

I take a consoling draught of coffee and burn my tongue.

※

D-Day, 18 March, comes and goes. Still no internet. Once again, I reach for my mobile.

I think I should fix up one of those prepaid funeral plans, just in case I commit harikari.

The only bright spot comes from the manager down at the Belstra shop. "I don't know what's going on," he says, "but take this little wireless modem. Just plug it in. Not fast, but it will keep you going."

Then—hooray! At last Belstra is really trying! Every five days now they send me text messages to tell me how hard they are working to fix my problem. And word has finally seeped through the impervious layers of Belstra bureaucracy into the mysterious caverns of the complaints department. They ring me. Twice. But both times the line drops out.

Silly me! I waste another ten minutes thinking they will ring back.

When I do make it to the end of one of the calls, there is a lovely little survey to complete. "Thinking about your call today," says the sweet recorded voice, "how likely would you be to recommend Belstra, when zero means 'not at all likely' and ten 'extremely likely'?" After I've stopped laughing, I try to enter minus five. She won't accept it.

※

Three months have passed. Still no cable internet. Nor has my central vision been healed. But the good thing about my eyes is that I feel no pain. That's more than I can say about Belstra. I might be legally blind, but when it comes to healing, there is a certain communications company that needs to be pushed right up to the head of the line.

I still believe in miracles ... but not the Belstra kind.

Keep five yards from a carriage,
ten yards from a horse,
and a hundred yards from an elephant;
but the distance one should keep from
a wicked man cannot be measured.
INDIAN PROVERB

FIFTY-FIVE

THE LAST WALI, THE MAD MULLAH AND MALALA

ADELAIDE, 2012

He claimed that the bullets of the British Raj would turn to water. He said his secret army was hidden in the hills, and he could feed them all with just a few grains of rice. He boasted he could make himself invisible. He lived a hundred years before Osama bin Laden, but they had a lot in common. Well-travelled, educated, intelligent, and able to stir up religious fervour against Western invaders.

The British called Saidullah "the Mad Mullah". He may have been crazy. He was certainly angry. That's because the British had invaded and drawn a line through his Pashtun tribes to demarcate Afghanistan and India, in an attempt to keep out the Russians' southward movement.

The Mullah's religious fervour reinforced his mystical claims and proved magnetic to the patriotic tribesmen of Swat. Together they attempted some dramatic attacks on the British. The young Winston Churchill was there, and I've seen the small fortress on a low hill they call "Churchill's Picket".

In the end the British bullets did not turn to water. The Mad Mullah had to back off when the tribes of the Swat ceased to support him.

*

Queen Elizabeth II called it "The Switzerland of the East". I am so glad that before my eyesight began to fade, I was able to enjoy the beautiful Valley of Swat. It was our family's favourite holiday destination.

Ice-blue mountain rivers. Swinging bridges. Green fields. Orchards. Summer peaches. Mistletoe forests. Horseshoes of water falls. Alpine lakes. Tasty trout. Snow-capped peaks. Glaciers. Wild strawberries. Twisting bazaars. Friendly villagers.

We loved to poke around in our favourite handicraft store. I remember our first visit: the aroma of polished, handcrafted wood, the clink of onyx chess sets and the dull gleam of brass samovar urns. Janna started admiring the softness and lightness of the Pashmina shawls.

The shopkeeper was watching. He stepped forward, took the shawls from Janna's hands and, in a "you haven't seen anything yet" tone, said, "Come upstairs. I have ordered tea."

We soon learned that upstairs was the place for serious customers. The clutter of pedestrian bric-a-brac was replaced by stacks and rolls of exotic handwoven carpets.

The shopkeeper waved a hand toward the centre of the room and seated the family in a half circle on a huge red and black carpet. The musty smell of ancient weaving soon mingled with the cardamom in the milky Kashmiri chai.

The proprietor turned to Janna. "You like Pashmina shawls, Memsahib?"

"*Bilkool Jhi*. Absolutely. They are so soft and light."

"Wait a moment," he said, "I have something to show you."

As he rose, a bunch of keys jingled in his hand. The correct key opened the lock on a sturdy wooden cupboard and he returned with a folded cloth. "This is our very best Pashmina," he said as he gently unfolded it and laid it in Janna's hands. Then he stood back and watched.

Her jaw dropped. "It's so light I can hardly feel it"—she looked up at our host—"yet it's so warm. It feels like melting butter."

When all the family had passed it round, the shopkeeper spoke quietly. "This costs more per ounce than gold." We all gasped. "The very finest fibres are the ones that are plucked, one by one, from the bushes along the wild goat trails."

We left the shop feeling as if we had handled the crown jewels.

But one thing that unsettled us on our Swat visits was having to detour around occasional roadblocks of burning tyres and fist-waving men. And in the Kalam bazaar, bearded men outside a small stone mosque were signing up Taliban recruits. Whenever I hear someone say "if looks could kill", my mind immediately takes me back to those penetrating eyes, surveying us from beneath dark turbans.

Yes, despite its beauty the Swat Valley is also known for its vulnerability to radical Islam. Gutsy Malala Yousafzai was a lover of the former and a victim of the latter. On 9 October 2012, a masked Taliban gunman stopped her school bus, called out her name and pulled the trigger.

But he couldn't shoot straight. The eleven-year-old survived the bullet through her skull and lived to become an international advocate for women's rights and girls' education. The attack backfired on the Taliban. Their very name means "students", but for them that only means male students. Females are excluded.

※

I never met the son of the last Wali of Swat, but my daughter nearly did. It happened during a 1985 boarding school break while Janna and I were working in the Thar Desert, a thousand miles to the south.

"Maria, you must come and stay with us," her red-haired classmate insists. "My dad always takes us to Swat this time of year. He has some projects up there. You might even meet the son of the last Wali of Swat."

A few years later we would move to the North-West Frontier and I would take over those projects from Susan's dad, who would retire back to England. But I didn't know that at the time.

Ten-year-old Maria is a bit confused. "Where's this place with the funny name?"

"It's a really beautiful valley. It takes a day to drive there from our place in Peshawar. It used to be a little mountain kingdom of its own. Dad says it was the last kingdom to be recognised in British India. He knows all about those things."

"And what is a Wali?"

"He was the last of their kings. Wali means 'ruler'. But he doesn't rule now, and he's very old. His son is a really nice man."

As it turns out, when Maria's host family reaches the Swat, Miangul Aurangzeb, the son of the Wali, is not at home. Susan's father frowns. "Hmm. He has a lot of political and business affairs that take him out of the valley." He strokes his greying ginger beard, then turns the key of his aging Land Rover. "We'll go and visit the Khan instead. I'll talk to him about the education projects."

Maria, who is more concerned about the conceited rat in *Charlotte's Web*, is still a bit confused. But all is explained to her on the way to the residence of the Khan, a lesser, but still important, valley dignitary. She learns that the aging Wali and his family are still very influential, even though the little kingdom is now part of Pakistan. And she learns that prior to serving tea, it is customary for a servant to pour each guest a glass of a red liquid with an unusual aroma.

In the Khan's reception room Maria and Susan are seated away from the chatting adults.

"What is this stuff? " Maria whispers. "It smells funny."

"It's *roohafza*. They drink it in hot weather. It's supposed to be refreshing."

Maria screws up her nose. "Smells like crushed ants to me. What does it taste like?"

"Try it if you want to," the redhead says, twisting her mouth. "I don't like it."

"So what do we do with it?"

Susan looks around and notes that the adults are all hard at it, nibbling small pieces of fried chicken and talking politics, projects and education. "This," she whispers, and she leans toward a large leafy pot plant. "I think it needs a drink, don't you?"

Maria extends her glass and follows suit. Moments later the servant notices the empty glasses and approaches with his jug and tray. The schoolgirls smile, shake their heads and sweetly decline.

So Maria never met the son of the last Wali of Swat. But when Janna and I moved from the desert to Peshawar, we found that one of his close relatives lived in a flat just below ours.

Janna loved to meet with Ayisha, a refined young woman with two smartly dressed small children.

"Ayisha is such a lovely person, Grant. And I love that perfume she buys on her trips to Dubai. Do you know she hangs all her clothes in big plastic bags to keep them out of all this black Peshawar pollution?"

"And I like Gul Muhammad's massive TV," I added.

Ayisha's husband was a farming landowner and we had a lot in common. He would invite me down to talk crops and watch cricket on his big-screen.

One day I arrive before the game starts. Gul Muhammad settles me into a well-upholstered lounge chair and we chat while a BBC interview burbles on.

The interviewee is a Western bishop. I pick up a bit of his drift, and suddenly I want to hear more.

I place a hand across my chest. "Please excuse me, Gul Muhammad. I must hear this man."

We both turn to the TV. My host is well-educated and soon picks up the cause of my interest and growing consternation. "Grant Jhi, don't you Christians believe that Rasool Isa Masih had a special birth? We believe that, too, but this man says it is not so. "

I nod and keep on listening. Now he is saying that Jesus Christ did not actually die and there was no resurrection.

Inside I'm churning. *Of course you're entitled to your views, mate, but how can you dress up in a Christian leader's garb and say such things? It's like a chess player saying he loves chess but doesn't believe in kings or knights. Or a mountain biker saying he doesn't believe in mountains. Or a footballer saying, "Let's play—we don't need the ball."*

I turn to my host. "You're a good Muslim, Gul Muhammad. If one of your religious leaders spoke up on TV and said things that were against the basics of Islam, what would you do?"

He looks a bit vacant, so I rephrase my question. "For example, if a Mullah said on television that Muhammad did not get any messages from the Angel Gabriel, and that he just made them all up, what would you do?"

Gul Muhammad launches his large frame out of his chair and points at the screen. "I would shoot the TV," he half shouts. Then he clenches his fists. "And I would go to the TV station, and I would shoot at the TV station."

The BBC interview finishes and the cricket coverage begins. Gul Muhammad reluctantly settles. If there is one thing he is more passionate about than his religion, it is his Pakistani cricket team. With enthusiasm he chastises the umpires, heckles the opposition and hands out advice to the players. But during the first tea break he leans toward me and gives me a surprise.

"What are you doing with your alcohol allowance, Grant Jhi?" he half whispers.

I am taken aback. All foreigners are allowed to go to a certain outlet and buy alcohol, but I haven't even thought about it. Yes, I have an occasional drink in Australia, but I've signed a statement saying I will respect the laws of my host country, the Islamic Republic of Pakistan.

"Gul Muhammad," I say, "I haven't done anything with it."

He brightens visibly. "You are not using any of it?"

I shake my head, and I realise that I am being backed into a corner. A corner where I do not want to be.

He smiles and leans closer. "Then we could come to a good arrangement. You can get your allowance, and I will pay you for it."

I know that many Muslims like alcohol, and if they drink it in private it is not a problem. They get their beer and whisky on the black market. But they are often disappointed with the quality. That's why my neighbour wants to get his hands on a better supply.

I don't want to get involved. If something went wrong, it could even affect my next visa. Yet I don't want to upset my neighbour. I had better find a way out—a way that does not ruin our good friendship.

A light bulb flashes in my brain. I smile inwardly and confidently turn to my host.

"Ah, Gul Muhammad, my dear friend," I say in a serious tone, "it is not lawful in your religion to consume alcohol." I pause to add sacred weight to my irrefutable argument. "I don't want to cause you to break your holy Islamic rules."

He smirks and replies in an equally confident tone, "Don't you worry about that, Mister Lock. Let *me* worry about that!"

I don't know how I did it, but somehow I managed to convince him, and we continued to be friends. But I sometimes wonder if alcohol became his regular companion. That's because his beautiful wife and two children were burnt to death in a bomb blast in a downtown clothing store. I think he could be excused for having to find solace in something.

Lovely Ayisha's royal relative, the last Wali of Swat, did not meet such a premature death. He lived until he was eighty. He was a progressive leader who built hospitals, schools and colleges. He was an early advocate for female education. If he had lived longer, it would have grieved him when the fundamentalists, with their strict sharia law, closed down the girls' schools.

But what a thrill it would have been for him if he had lived to see Malala survive her attack and go on to be an international advocate for education, particularly for girls. And what a thrill to know that a daughter of his Swat Valley addressed the United Nations, became the youngest recipient of a Nobel Peace Prize, and for three consecutive years has been listed as one of the top one hundred most influential people in the world.

FIFTY-SIX

JULIETTA

ADELAIDE, 2012

Julietta points with Italian exuberance. "Look at the birds, Alonzo! Aren't they beautiful? We don't see birds like that in Dubai."

The toddler runs toward the Aussie magpies, making similar squawks in a mixture of Italian, English and Filipino. Spanish is not included in the babble. Although he has a Mexican birth certificate, he only heard Spanish for the first two weeks of his life, until Julietta and her Australian husband adopted him. They all moved into a UN residence in the United Arab Emirates, along with the Filipino nanny.

What a mix, I am thinking as his mother shares the family story.

"My husband has restored so many limbs, saved so many lives, with his plastic surgery." She waves her arms. "Afghanistan, Iraq, Pakistan. The UN sends us wherever there are bomb blasts. We work together as a team."

"A team?"

"Yes. I am a microsurgeon. I join the severed nerves and tissue, but my husband … he is brilliant." Her hands go to her lips, then skyward. *"Magnifico!"*

Janna and I often walk along this bush track in the rugged Morialta Gorge. So close to Adelaide City, but so outback in feel. And you never know who you might meet. Last week it was a family of Afghan asylum seekers. They were surprised when we addressed them in their Dari language. Today it is Julietta and two-year-old Alonzo. We pause beside them to enjoy those brilliant baubles of the bush, the rainbow lorikeets, feeding only a few feet away.

"Look, Alonzo! Look at these birds! Look at the colour!" She turns our way. "In Dubai we only see Indian mynas."

Janna loves her Italian accent. We soon learn that Julietta is not happy with the Australian Government.

"They are so rude." Her hands are waving again. "It is as though we have done something wrong applying for Alonzo to become an Australian. I am an Aussie citizen now, but I am not proud of this bureaucratic Australian Government."

She stands erect. "In Italy they recognised him straight away. Italy has many drawbacks, but at least they appreciate family."

Now it's Janna's turn to wave her hands. "Our daughter and her husband worked in Indonesia and adopted a little Indonesian boy. That was seven years ago and they're still waiting for Leonardo's Australian passport. The red tape, the paperwork—it's never ending!"

Then I speak up. "I don't understand it. Thousands of people have flown into this country on tourist visas, and when they expire they just lay low and stay here. But legitimate adoptions by Australian citizens have to wait years to be validated."

We roll our eyes. Julietta dives at her toddler as he wobbles off the path, then renews her diatribe.

"They have started the process, but there are so many hurdles."

I take Alonzo and swing him between my legs. He makes happy noises.

"It is only because we are well educated, and both surgeons, that they even listen to us," Julietta says. "And because they want us back here one day, after we finish with the UN."

"That's interesting," says Janna as she takes a turn at entertaining the boy. "They've sent you to some of the places where we've worked, like Pakistan and Afghanistan."

In between steering the empty pusher with one hand and pointing at birds with the other, Julietta asks about our twenty-four years of input into community development and empowering the poor.

She stops and looks squarely at us. "I am so happy to meet you. We are front-line workers. When there is an emergency, we are in and then out. But you are the ones who serve the people and train them long-term. And I am so glad you worked with the women, Janna. Their lives are so difficult in those Islamic countries."

"Tell me about it," says Janna. "It's not good to be born a woman in those places."

Julietta leans forward. "Can I tell you a story? A true story?"

We nod.

"Have you been to Kandahar in Afghanistan?"

"Yes. We had projects there."

"There was a bomb blast," Julietta says. "A Taliban roadside bomb. I worked on this woman's legs, or what was left of them, for twelve hours. My fingers were getting so tired. Then they started cramping and losing their feeling, but I went on and finished my work. Then I said, 'Now this woman must go to my husband for the plastic surgery. I have done all I can.'"

"The interpreter explained to her husband, and the husband said, 'No! This cannot happen.'"

"'Why not?' I said. 'If she doesn't have the skin surgery, she will die.'"

"He pointed at me and said, 'You! *You* do it!'"

"'But I *cannot* do it,' I told him. 'It is not my field. My husband is a specialist in this work.'"

"He just stuck out his beard and said, 'No man will look at my wife! No man will touch my wife! It is against our belief. *You* must do it!'"

"I was so angry that I shouted at him. 'Listen, man! Do you not care for your wife? She is the mother of your eight children. She will die if my husband does not do the surgery. Do you want that? Do you want her to die?'"

"'No man will look at my wife!' he said, and he walked away."

"I pleaded with the interpreter. He just shrugged."

"So what happened?"

Julietta clenches her fists. "She died! It makes me so angry."

Janna lets out a sigh. "I could tell you many stories too. Like Dr Wazir in the delivery rooms of a hospital in Kabul. He was the one who butchered poor Afia—without an anaesthetic!"

The microsurgeon is shaking her head. "How Islam can say it is a religion of compassion and peace, and respects women, I will never know."

"When it comes to human rights, it has a long way to go," I add. "It's still in the grip of a male-dominated, Middle Eastern culture from the seventh century. Yet they tell us they look after their women. And these are the countries which have had Islam the longest." I pause. "It makes me think of the old Afghan proverb, 'Don't show me the palm tree, show me the dates.'"

Julietta looks at her watch and gasps. "I have to go. We fly out tomorrow morning." She battles to strap Alonzo into the pusher. She quickly takes our email address and turns back toward the car park.

Janna and I walk on in silence.

Finally, Janna speaks. "I hope we meet Julietta again."

FIFTY-SEVEN

TSUNAMI

ADELAIDE, 2012

What kind of God is this?

But have you ever thanked him
for the kiss
of morning sun
rising on purple-headed mountains?

Earthquakes!
He must be a God of death!

But have you ever thanked him
for each breath
your diaphragm automatically takes
when you're fast asleep?
And when you are awake?

Fire, flood, drought!
Uncaring God!

I hear your shout,
but do you ever pause
to give him praise
for all the years
and months and days
that thus far
you've been given?

Earth trembles in resonant grief.

"Remember me, Lord!" cries the thief
Crowd jeers
He fights for breath
High priest leers
Sun bows its head
Yes, we all must face
the sting of death.

Spear pierces corpse's side.
Ha, that's the end of him!
Dismal, deluded liar. He lied,
Said he could forgive our sin,
Thought he was God. Crazy clown!
Did you see how he looked at that thief
and *grinned?*

On the third day, he rose from the dead,
Drew near, smiled and said,
I am Life,
Come, enjoy my wine!
Celebrate! Suffer!
Share my bread!
And now I know
he's the ever-green vine
and I am forever his twig.

And that's big man!

Really big.

FIFTY-EIGHT

THE LEFT SIDE

ADELAIDE, 2011

"The men's toilet, Grant?"

"Yes."

"That's easy," my colleague whispers. "Just go back into the foyer and it's on your left side."

The annual synod meeting has adjourned for lunch and there is always a rush on the toilets. I quietly slide my chair back while the archbishop is still praying: "And we thank you, Lord, for your goodness and for the food we are about to enjoy." I join in with a hearty "Amen" and I am on my way.

There is always that thirty-second or so pause before a crowd starts to surge. This smug delegate will have the men's rest room to himself.

I'm through into the foyer and turning left, just like he told me. You have to be a bit proactive when you are visually impaired. It's ironic. If it wasn't for this central vision blindness, I could still be director of a huge eye-care program in Afghanistan. But at least I still have peripheral vision. Can't see the koala, but I can see the tree. Can't see the face, but I can see the person. Can't read the writing, but I can still see the book. I'm thankful for that.

That's it, turn left and follow that guy in the black trousers. He must be an early bird like me. Ah, plenty of cubicles in here. I'll take the one at the far end, on the left.

I enter and lock myself in. Moments pass.

Hey, the walls must be pretty thin! I can hear the chitchat of women in the female toilets. They sure are an animated bunch. They sound like they're just outside my cubicle door.

Oh, no!

My arms hang heavy. My legs go weak. No wonder I didn't pass any urinals on the way in! I'm trapped, like a criminal caught in a spotlight.

But hold on, they don't know I'm in here. I'll just stay put. I won't open that door till they are all gone. No one will know, and no one will talk.

Don't be a dummy. Over half of the three hundred delegates are women, and the break lasts for an hour. What kind of pervert would linger all lunch hour in a women's rest room? And listen to the noise out there—the numbers are swelling. Someone is sure to tap on the cubicle door.

Well, I argue back, I could just call out in a falsetto voice "Won't be long, dear!" and keep the door shut.

You've got to do better than that, Grant. Hey, it's a genuine mistake. Why not just walk out?

My embarrassed muscles won't move.

Wait a minute! Back in Pakistan, a man climbing to the flat-roof of his house has to keep shouting, "Man on the roof! Man on the roof!" That way he won't be accused of looking over the wall at his neighbour's women. They will all scurry from their high-walled courtyards into the *purdah* of their mud-brick homes.

OK. That's it. I take a deep breath and call out loudly from my cubicle, "Man in the room! Man in the room!"

The chattering stops. There is a chorus of a cappella gasps. I go on quickly, "It's all a mistake. I'm visually impaired. I came to the wrong place and I'm leaving. Right now!"

With that, I press the flush button, burst out of the cubicle. The waiting group parts like the Red Sea. I wish I was back there with Moses and his trusty staff, and not here with my skinny white cane, all these skirts and, yes, a few pairs of black trousers.

There is a kindly feminine snigger: "You'd have to be a brave man to come in here."

"Nothing to do with bravery," I spout as I stride out into the foyer, desperately hoping that everyone out there is looking the other way.

Peripherally, I glimpse a stream of trousers heading for another door, a bit further along. And yes, it's also on the left side.

FIFTY-NINE

FINDING THE MASTERMIND

ABBOTTABAD, 2011

High walls surround all the homes in Abbottabad. That's normal in Pakistan. You need them to protect your property, your privacy and your women. But on the top of one of the bumpy green hills that punctuate this northern town, there was a three-storey mansion with walls much higher than the rest. Few were allowed to enter.

In the nearby tea house the locals quietly compared notes on their secretive neighbours.

"Funny how we never see them."

"The only visitors they have come at night."

"Must be one of those wealthy drug dealers from Waziristan."

"Better not to ask questions."

It was all a mystery until one moonless night in May 2011. The sound of Black Hawk helicopters broke the silence, and US Navy SEALs dropped in on Osama bin Laden.

It looked like a Hollywood movie. But this was no more an invention of Hollywood than 9/11.

※

I did a lot of legal work in Abbottabad. I worked with a local lawyer to prevent an government department from taking land from a minority group. Musadiq Quazi used to be a fighter pilot in Pakistan's air force. I often wondered if the scars high on his forehead were the result of some aeronautical misadventure. Then he told me he got them in the most dangerous place in Pakistan—on the roads. His Mercedes sedan was solid and no doubt saved him.

To resolve the dispute I visited the army's training academy in Abbottabad. Abbottabad has always been a military town. It was founded by Major James Abbott back in the days of British rule. These days it is the

West Point, or Duntroon, of the Pakistan Army. That same army was receiving money from America to help root out the al-Qaeda terrorists operating from the mountains on the Afghan border. And there, right in their midst, was al-Qaeda's leader, the 9/11 mastermind, the man with the world's biggest bounty on his head: USD$25 million. Did the intelligence arm of the army know he was there? Many think they did.

The British influence hangs on. In a reception room of Abbottabad's administrator, I was greeted by a cheerful clerk. Gulzar Khan gave me a toothy grin from behind his enormous typewriter. It soon became clear that he thought I was his ticket to something or somewhere. He ordered tea and insisted on taking my address.

I later received a letter containing a distinctly Victorian tone:

> Mr Grant Lock Sahib
>
> I am exceedingly grateful to see Your Laudable honour at Abbottabad. In fact I have no words to express my gratitude for your laudable honour. I have full faith that your honour very kindly maintain fraternization with me for all time to come.

He then proceeded to request assistance in gaining an American visa, and concluded with:

> Kindly accept my heartiest compliments and also pay my compliments to all your honour's kith and kin.
>
> Gulzar Khan son of Late Akhram Khan

I replied politely, advising him I was not in a position to help with any visa applications to America.

I also thought that being addressed as "your laudable honour" was elevating me beyond my station. Apparently I was wrong. His second letter arrived just before Christmas, tapped out on that same ancient typewriter.

> The Most Honourable Grant H. Lock
>
> Kindly accept my heartiest congratulation on Christmas/ New Year and the recipient of Good wishes.

This is sending Your Majesty felicitations for a Christmas/ New Year that's happy and merry all thro. I pray for Your honour everlasting pleasures and happiness.

I have full faith that you would very kindly maintain these fraternal relation for all time to cone with me. I earnestly wish that you and yours would be the recipient of the choicest blessing of Almighty Allah forever.

Yours affectionately,

Gulzar Khan son of Late Akhram Khan

As a member of Gulzar's self-appointed royal family, I did have the opportunity to drink tea with him one more time. Although Australia did not interest him, I have occasionally wondered if kindly Gulzar was ever successful in reaching the United States. With his anachronistic type-writing background, I doubt he would have ever graduated to word processing in New York. But if he had, he may have been one of the nearly three thousand souls who perished when Osama bin Laden's suicide pilots flew their flights of terror.

A huge wave of American fear, indignation and anger rose with the smoke and dust. A decade and a half later, the hurt goes on.

Recently Janna and I had a stopover in Hong Kong. "We need exercise," she said. On the way down in the lift we chit-chatted with some Americans. "Yes," I said, "we were in Islamic countries for twenty-four years," and I handed a woman a *Shoot Me First* card.

We were halfway to the pool when we heard the sound of high-heels running. A woman's voice called out, "I have to buy this book. I have to read it." We turned and she stopped in front of us, waving the card in my face. Then she whispered, "I am from New York. I was there on September 11."

※

When the helicopters left Abbottabad with the body of Osama bin Laden, Pakistan was furious. How dare the Americans fly into their airspace? There were demonstrations on the streets. Diplomatic anger was vented.

But hold on. Shouldn't they be pleased that the mastermind of terror has been eliminated? If al-Qaeda flourishes, are they not in line to suffer more terrorism themselves? And what would happen if the terrorists set their sights on controlling Pakistan's nuclear arsenal?

We now know the Americans did not trust their Pakistani partners in the war on terror. If they had, the Mastermind may somehow have been tipped off.

But how were the Americans so sure that the man they were looking for was in that seldom-visited walled mansion on one of Abbottabad's hills. Even when their suspicions were raised by tracking a certain courier, they couldn't be sure. Satellites and stakeouts didn't produce unequivocal results.

It all came down to a nurse's needle.

Dr Shakil Afridi was recruited. "Run a vaccination campaign in Abbottabad," he was instructed. "When your nurse is let through those gates, get her to suck a bit of DNA out of the kids while she's doing the vaccination job." Then they matched the DNA of the Mastermind's children with that of some of his cooperative Saudi family. Bingo, they knew he was there.

As soon as the raid was over, the Americans rang Pakistan and announced that its airspace had been violated. Yes, Pakistan was furious. But on the other hand, hadn't they promised to join the search for bin Laden? And wouldn't you think that, after the dust settled, Dr Shakil Afridi would get a medal from the Pakistani Government for his local input into the success of the operation? But no—they handed him a thirty-three year jail sentence. I've visited Pakistani prisons. They are not nice places.

Nowadays, so much depends on Afghanistan and Pakistan getting along like good neighbours. It is slow in happening. Tens of millions of war-weary citizens live in the hope of positive negotiations.

Pakistan holds the trump cards. Landlocked Afghanistan can easily be snookered by Pakistan's closing the border and shutting off access to its big port at Karachi. Thousands of trucks would bank up on each side of the closed border gate. Afghanistan would rapidly start to choke.

The other trump card in Pakistan's hand is the several million Afghan refugees still living in Pakistan. They have been pushed out by thirty-five years of conflict, beginning with the Russian invasion in the 1970s. Pakistan could say, "That's it! Regardless of what the UN says, we're sending them back." With unemployment running at possibly more than fifty percent in Afghanistan, how would the Afghan government manage?

As politicians continue to point their fingers, tongues and even guns across their respective borders, things look grim.

Most of the foreign troops have now left Afghanistan. They tried to make it sound like a victory, but terrorism continues on both sides of the border. Bin Laden's al-Qaeda has been weakened but is still around. Islamic State has arrived. And the Taliban continue to be a major headache for both countries.

Every stone strikes the feet of the poor.
AFGHAN PROVERB

SIXTY

TWO DOLLARS' WORTH

KABUL, 2005

Tears come to the Afghan woman's eyes. "I am pregnant."
Janna is excited. "*Tarbreek! Tarbreek!* Congratulations, Marzia!" She hugs her visitor.
But the pregnant woman's body is stiff. Unresponsive.
"Janna Jaan, dear Janna, I must have fifty Afghanis."
Janna knows that her Marzia is not the asking type. Fifty Afghanis is less than $2. "What is it for, Marzia? A check-up?"
The younger woman struggles to look her proxy mother in the eye. She touches her body as though it carries a disease and whispers, "I have to get rid of it."

※

Janna first met Marzia soon after we moved across town to the suburb of Aloudin, close to our Kabul headquarters. She was the first person to receive my wife into the neighbourhood.
"Grant! I had a lovely welcome today."
"From whom?" I ask as I adjust our fickle diesel heater.
"She must be one of the poorest women around. But she was lovely. And she only had rubber flip-flops on her feet."
"That's not good with all the snow," I reply. "Time to eat?"
We move to the table for our evening meal. This is a good part of the day, when we share our daily ups and downs. Janna talks about her team member pastoral care and widows' work, and I talk about the development projects I am involved in.
"I met her when I was taking the shortcut to the office," Janna says. "The park looks like fairy-land, with the pine trees all covered with snow."
"Looks good now," I mumble, "but in the summer it's a dust-bowl, and it'll be a mud-bath when the snow melts."

Janna ignores me and proceeds to serve the spinach and potato curry. "She had two ragamuffin kids with her, and she was taking them to the *Parwishghar*, the orphanage. You know, the large compound at the end of our block."

I nod. "Yeah, the one with the big flat roof where the security soldiers post a lookout and a sniper whenever some dignitary is on the way to Parliament House."

Janna passes a bowl to me. She pauses. "Grant, I was horrified that she had to give up her little children. You know how I love kids."

"Is she a widow?"

"No, she's not. She has an old grey-beard as a husband. Apparently, the kids only go for the day."

"So orphanages here take kids who aren't orphans? That's interesting."

"Marzia told me that because they are so poor, she can take her little boy and girl in the morning and collect them in the afternoon. They get a free meal and some teaching."

I reach for another piece of warm naan bread, fresh from the tandoor shop at the end of the street. "That's good. What do they learn?"

Janna rolls her eyes. "Marzia says they learn to sweep, clean and wash things. There are hundreds of kids there—not surprising after nearly thirty years of war."

I tear off a piece of the flat bread and shape it into a small edible scoop, Afghan-style. "Sounds like they only get that meal if they work for it. But that's better than starving, despite what the West might say about child labour."

"Oh," Janna says, "they're not her only kids. She has six altogether. And she's not going to have any more. '*Bayshuck!*' she said. 'Definitely not!'"

But Marzia is not the first to make that statement and then feel the nausea of morning sickness.

※

There is desperation in Marzia's eyes as she repeats her words in a whisper. "Janna Jaan, I *have* to get rid of it."

"But Marzia!"

The Afghan woman raises her hand and pours out the logic of her poverty. "We are very poor, Janna Jaan. My husband can't get work. My oldest son finds a little but not enough. There are already eight of us. How can we feed another mouth?" She tightens her fists. "I *have* to do it! Again!"

"What do you mean, Marzia? *What* do you have to do again?"

Then it all comes out.

Marzia has already been to a doctor. He gave her medicine guaranteed to remove the baby. But the guarantee failed. She had to buy more medicine. She scrounged and lied to her white-bearded husband to put enough money together.

"The second time, I was so sick I thought I would die. But it's still there! Now I have no more money, Janna Jaan. But I *have* to get rid of it!"

Janna knows how much Afghans love their children. Knows how hard it has been for her visitor to take this course. "But, Marzia, you have tried twice now. Perhaps ... perhaps this is a special baby."

"Please, Janna Jaan, help me. It is for the best."

Janna is struggling. She reads the pain and resolve in the young woman's gaze. *What can I do? I've never been asked to finance an abortion before. This is one roleplay we didn't rehearse during our cross-cultural training back in civilised Melbourne.*

"I'll tell you what I will do," she hears herself saying. "I will give you the money, Marzia, and I will pray with you." She takes her visitor's work-worn hands into her own. "But remember, Marzia Jaan, this could be a special baby."

After her visitor leaves, Janna can't stop mulling.

It's a crazy world. Back in Australia, a country struggling to grow its population, the unborn are conveniently disposed of. And, if a couple want to adopt a child, it's as difficult as forcing a camel through the eye of the proverbial needle. In all Australia, there are only a few hundred adoptions a year and the number is falling, while the wait time for adopting overseas children is five years and rising.

I love to see all the children here in Afghanistan, but oversized families are a huge challenge. What can be done to encourage family planning? Husbands, religious leaders and cultural expectations are all against it. Add ignorance, illiteracy, poverty, war and high child mortality and it's all uphill. Still, the old Afghan proverb says, "There is a path to the top of even the highest mountain." The government does have some family planning clinics, and other organisations also help. And our big team contributes with female clinics, community development and capacity building across the country. But climbing that mountain is tough going. There are too many heavy rocks in the backpack.

A month later, Marzia returns. Her skinny frame and baggy clothing give no clue to the success or failure of the two dollars' worth of Afghanis.

"Come in, Marzia, come in," Janna says.

The young woman slips her shoes off outside the door and Janna leads her to the *toshak* cushions in our living room. "I've just made tea."

She brings another cup and settles beside her guest. "Tell me how it went, Marzia. Are you OK?" She reaches for the teapot. "Did the medicine fail again, for the third time?"

"No, it didn't."

Janna pauses.

"I didn't take it."

"You didn't take it?"

"You were right, Janna Jaan." Marzia lays a hand on her abdomen and gives a slight smile.

Janna leans forward. "Marzia, tell me. What happened?"

"The doctor took my pulse, and then he said it was too late. He gave the money back and said exactly what you said: 'This must be a special baby.' " She reaches into the folds of her clothing. "Here is the money, Janna Jaan."

Janna puts down the teapot. *There is something about this ragged young woman. How many others would bring the money back to me? They would just say they paid for the medicine and it didn't work. Or just not show up again.*

She hugs her friend. "You must keep it, Marzia, for the sake of your baby. Your special baby!"

SIXTY-ONE

THE CRAB GIRL

KABUL, 2005

Tap, tap. Tap, tap, tap.

It's Marzia, frantically knocking on our gate. She has forgotten we have a bell to press.

Mirwais, our Hazara helper, is cutting grass in the garden and shows her in.

She is not alone. Clinging to her mother's skirts is six-year-old Parwana, her eyes opaque with terror.

Janna has been slogging through some language revision and now she knows why our organisation puts us through the pain. Somehow she has always been able to express compassion for the poor, but local words add so much more.

"Marzia Jaan! Che gup-as?—What is the matter?"

"It's Parwana," Marzia pants. "She must stay here. Oh please, Janna Jaan. She cannot go back to my house."

Janna kneels and tries to keep calm. "Parwana, dear, what's the matter?"

Mirwais appears. "Shall I bring chai?"

Whimpering, Parwana scuttles behind her mother. Her small fists, like white-knuckled crab-pincers, close on Marzia's skirts.

Janna notes the reaction. *She's not hiding from me, she's hiding from Mirwais. She's hiding from men.*

"*Ballay,* Mirwais. Yes, make tea," Janna says. Sickle still in hand, the young man heads for the kitchen, and the small crab-girl slowly relaxes her grip.

Janna recognises Parwana's attire. The pink *shalwar* suit stood out in the second-hand bazaar from all the others she bought for needy girls.

"Parwana, you still have that nice *shalwar kamiz* outfit. It looks so pretty on you."

The compliment doesn't work.

"Parwana, tell me. What is the matter?"

Marzia takes her daughter's shoulders. "Let go, Parwana." She twists the girl around. The little girl turns, her terrorised eyes crab-stalking out from her head. Her mother pulls the *dupatta* scarf from her daughter's neck.

Janna's hand goes to her mouth as two purple-red welts, the thickness of rope, appear on the front of the little girl's neck. "What happened?" she gasps. "Who did this?"

Marzia ignores the question. "She has to stay here with you, Janna Jaan."

"Someone tried to strangle her," Janna says. "I can see it, Marzia. Who did it?"

Marzia says nothing.

There is a light tap on the door. "*Chai tayarus*—The tea is ready," announces Mirwais, tray in hand.

Janna sees the little crab-fists grab at her mother's skirts once again.

"Thanks, Mirwais. That will be all." As soon as he is gone, she eyeballs her guest and continues the interrogation.

"A man did this, Marzia. A man stood behind this poor little girl and tried to strangle her with a rope or something."

No answer.

"Why, Marzia?"

No answer.

"Was it your husband?"

Marzia's eyes flicker, but no answer.

Janna's mind is in overdrive. *That guy is old enough to be your grandfather, Marzia. I don't know why you married him. But then, you had no say in it. Your family was poor. His first wife had died and he had some money. Now he seldom gets work. Just sits around the house giving orders. If only there were some real authorities here to report such things to. But if there were, they would probably be run by men. And like the police, they would only listen to Marzia's old husband. Age deserves respect over youth. Men deserve respect over women. Doesn't their book say that a woman's testimony is only worth half that of a man's?*

Marzia's eyes are searching her hostess's face for a sign of hope. Inside, Janna is churning with anger, compassion and shared vulnerability. She takes Marzia's hands and begins to speak. Her words bring pain to them both.

"I would love to have Parwana for a while, Marzia. But you know what would happen. Your men would be around here tomorrow. They would bring the police, and we know whose side the police would take. And they would complain to the Ministry of the Interior. I could lose my visa. We could be thrown out. What good would that be? Rest awhile, and I will send some beans and flour back with you. And I will pray."

Then she adds, "You must keep Parwana close to you at all times."

Marzia's face acknowledges the truth of her situation.

"But remember, Marzia Jaan, my teapot is always ready for you." Janna turns to the little girl. "And Parwana, remember that your name means 'butterfly', and that you will always be my pretty butterfly. Always."

And the little crab-girl almost smiles.

Every now and then, Marzia takes up Janna's invitation.

"Things are just too much, Janna Jaan. My husband is angry because I do not supply him with the right kind of food. Yet he gives me so little money."

"Janna Jaan, I had to get out of the house or I would go crazy. Back in the village, my husband's family was threatened by the Taliban. Now there are seventeen of us, in just two rooms. But we cannot turn away family—there will surely be a time when we need them!"

Sometimes, Marzia brings her special baby boy, but always Parwana comes with her. The purple marks on the butterfly crab-girl's neck gradually fade, as does the terror in her eyes. But those who know will always be able to detect the scars of both.

There will always be questions.

SIXTY-TWO

HUBBLE IMAGES

ADELAIDE, 2011

Swirling, curling Andromeda,
deep-field galaxies.
I pause and I wonder:
Why is there something
instead of nothing?

Intergalactic nebulae.
Black holes. Supernovas.
Endless uncharted skies.
And I ponder:
Who am I?

Am I just a meaningless microbe
on a miniscule globe
orbiting a speck called the sun?
Needle in a hay-filled stadium,
golf ball on a zillion zillion hole course,
shooting star without a source?

I feel so insignificant
so small.
Just a flash without meaning.
And at the end of the maze
a wall
with wasted screaming.

What is this dance we are in?
And what of us, the dancers?
I have the questions,
but who has the answers?

So
I shuffle along the nowhere line.

The visitor gives an invitation
"Come, let me show you eternity
my playground
my banquet hall
and your lost destination."

"Me, Sir?
Do you really mean me?"

"Absolutely!
But other voices have drowned my call,
and you've been blind
to who you really are.
But I've prepared the way,
so come."

Wait, Sir!
What should I bring?"

"Bring?
You can't bring anything.
Leave the baggage
and with many friends
we'll run free.
Life's not meant to have an end."

But, Sir, I can't see you,
and yet I feel your force.
I don't understand.

"My son,
Read the scrolls.
Take my hand.
You are mine.
I *am* the Source.
All is ready
So come.
My name is
Forever.
Let's run!"

Like cold water to a weary soul
is good news from a distant land.
HEBREW PROVERB

SIXTY-THREE

THE MUDDY MORGUE

KIMBA, A YEAR WITHOUT RAIN

She had to get a drink, along with the rest of the mob. But the dam is drying out. Now she is bogged.
    Did she rush in too quickly? Misjudge where the firmness gave away to ooze? Or was she bumped by other thirsty drinkers? They're all gone now. Back over the bank and into the paddock with their lambs.

*

The drought is on. As one dam dries up, the boss moves the mob to another dusty paddock, with another shallow pool. They all have mud on the bottom. Unforgiving clay. He looks toward the west. Not a cloud in sight and nothing in the long-range forecast. Only one more dam after this one, and not much in the bottom of that.
    Before that last one dries out he'll have to ring the agent, who'll ring the truckers. In a drought, you give them away. A lot of trucks are heading for the abattoirs these days. Feed has gone. Water has gone. Top breeders, too. The re-stockers aren't interested: the drought's too widespread.
    She pushes back. Sinks deeper. Tries to turn. Sinks deeper. After nine hours of intermittent struggle, there is no hope. A fleece of wool can keep out showers, heat and cold, but it can't keep out this water. There is no way she can lift double her

sodden weight. It's getting hard to hold her head above the muddy morgue.

And now the crows have come. Land on her head. Drive their beaks towards her eyes. Not a big meal, but tasty pickings. She won't have the strength to throw them off for much longer.

Back in the mob, her lamb calls out. No answer. There is only so long a young lamb can hang on without its mother's milk. And if it tries to filch from another mother, there will be a quick sniff from the ewe and a mighty thump from her rear hoof. Ewes know their lambs. Know their bleat and know their smell.

The sun sinks lower and lower, as does her head.

The crows are the first to hear the distant drum of the diesel engine. They leap into the air as the boss's ute bursts up and over the bank. He doesn't scan for long. "Trouble here, Blue!" he shouts. "You stay! Don't want you upsetting her." The dog leans out from the tray, but doesn't leap. "She's in deep, Blue. A long way out. Nearly had it. Looks like it's all the way with this one."

Blue whimpers in agreement. Tongue lolling, eyes keen, he really wants to help. But the order is to stay.

The boss yanks at his boots. "Hold on, girl! Hold on!" He peels off his socks. Click—he releases his belt. He throws jeans, jocks and shirt through the open door of the ute and strides toward the mud.

He's up to his waist in it. Outstretched arms. Gentle hands. Firm voice. "Come on, girl. You're gonna make it."

SIXTY-FOUR

FACES OF DEATH

ADELAIDE, 2014

I lie here like a broken brick.
    I see their faces. I recall their love for serving the Afghan people. Now their bullet-ridden bodies lie in some dingy morgue. But they need to get back to Finland, their home.
    It's not fair, Lord! It's not right!
    It was just another shopping trip to the bazaar. But it was during Ramzan. In that month of the fast, does not Allah forgive manifold sins if nothing passes your lips during daylight hours? And is there not an extra blessing for brave jihadi warriors who eliminate unbelieving *kafirs*?
    The two men spot the old taxi that the foreign women regularly use. This is going to be easy, like shooting fish in a barrel. The well-covered fish are clearly visible in the back seat.
    A motorbike with a pillion passenger draws alongside the taxi, then moves closer. The pillion rider raises his arm and the automatic weapon spews death.
    It is all over. The brave soldiers of God have gone.
    And so have our former colleagues.

※

My phone rings at 2.00 am. It is my daughter calling from Melbourne. "Dad, I've got bad news," she says.
    A busy mother of three, Maria doesn't have time to watch the TV bulletins. But while four-month-old Ryan is feeding, she gets out her smart-phone and checks the internet headlines. "I've just read it on the BBC News site, Dad. Two foreign women, aid workers, gunned down in Afghanistan. Happened an hour ago."

My grip tightens on the phone. The faces of colleagues back in Afghanistan flash through my mind. Which ones took the bullets? The hatred? The anger? I don't want to hear the details. I don't want to hear the names. But I have to ask.

"Did they say where, Maria?"

"Herat, Dad."

Immediately I know they were working in the Primary Mental Health Care Program. I used to be the Project Director for that dynamic program. And after thirty-five years of conflict, terrorism, displacement and destruction, who needs primary mental health care more than Afghanistan?

The ones who face the hardest struggle are the women. Those tough, anonymous women of Afghanistan. But even the most resilient can crack under the strain of widow-making wars. And when the rain and snow fail, it could mean you and your children have to survive on grass. You watch their bellies grow large and their limbs grow thin. And there is always the strain of being an Afghan woman, an unappreciated but essential pillar of a misogynistic society. Islam says women are only belongings. They can't think and they are disposable. They must go on doing what their mothers and grandmothers did. It is ordained. If you are born a woman, this is your lot. And if you do not produce sons, it will be worse for you.

Some can't take it any more. They don't realise that, if they found their way to that large white building on a stony rise just outside of Herat, there would be someone to listen. Someone to care. Instead they reach for the matches and the can of kerosene. Half has gone into the round burner to cook the daal and vegetables, and the other half will immolate the cook. The worn-out mother. The harassed, battered wife. The smell of the garments soaked in distilled petroleum gives way to the violent heat of the flames. And if the flames do not do their work, the hospital infections will complete the job.

If only someone had cared. If only someone had listened.

But there *was* someone who cared. Someone who could listen. Someone who could supply wise counsel and simple antidepressants to help get through the dark valley.

Now two of those "someones" have gone.

Will the primary mental health care program collapse? Funding has been hard to come by lately. The Japanese Government has helped with the buildings, but it is hard to get support for running costs. And these people are so poor. They can't pay much. The enthusiastic team of Afghan colleagues, young doctors, nurses and university graduates, all need a wage. And they need on-going training, encouragement and leadership. Now two-thirds of that leadership has gone, gunned down by the bullets of bigoted arrogance. Bullets of blindness.

The third remains. Our friend Katrin, the sweet, competent, professional Finnish volunteer.

Yesterday, Katrin expected her two friends to return from shopping, chatting about the clothes in the bazaar and opening up a box of Iranian-style confectionary. But only their ghosts will unpack the groceries. Only their ghosts will share the summer grapes, the red-ripe pomegranates and the tarbooza melons. Ghosts are silent. Their empty forms can never replace the reality of huggable bodies, Finnish voices and common companionship.

And if Katrin returns to Finland, can the Afghan staff keep the doors open for people like Keemia?

There is a doorway that
connects two hearts.
AFGHAN PROVERB

SIXTY-FIVE

KEEMIA

HERAT, 2007

I am flying west from Kabul to Herat across the entire width of Afghanistan, snow-covered mountains all the way. It is a regular visit to support our primary mental health team.

Coming through the doors, I pass an Afghan woman. Her glance flashes personal esteem and quiet confidence.

In Katrin's office, I ask, "Who was that women we just passed? Is she staff?"

Katrin smiles a satisfied smile and shakes her head. "Keemia came to us a year ago. She had been tossed out by her husband and his family."

"Why? She looks so young."

Katrin gestures toward a chair. I sit as she continues.

"Keemia has epileptic fits. She would roll on the floor, jerking her limbs and nearly passing out. They thought that she was faking it to get attention. Or that it was a *djinn*, an evil spirit. Her mother-in-law was angry. Perhaps she felt cheated that she did not know about this until after the arranged marriage went through. She made life even harder for the girl. You know how it is, Grant, when the new bride goes to live with the husband's family."

I did know. All over Pakistan and Afghanistan, the mother-in-law rules, and the newcomer can be treated like a servant. Some young women become so stressed and starved of attention and value that, somehow, they force themselves to faint.

"So what did the mother-in-law do?"

"The next time Keemia had a fit, she threw boiling water over her legs—to drive out the *djinn*, or to prove she was faking it."

"What happened?"

"Nothing. Nothing but huge blisters."

"And?"

"Her husband divorced her on the spot. They threw her out and sent her back to her family. Her father is a flower gardener. He sells his produce in the bazaar."

"But how did she get here, Katrin?"

"They heard about us from the neighbours. Out of desperation, her father finally brought her to us. We isolated the problem, counselled her and put her on some simple medication."

"That's great," I say, "and she looked so full of confidence."

"Yes, now she has hope." Katrin smiles. "And she has just become engaged to marry another man."

SIXTY-SIX

THE AFGHAN WEDDING AND THE DRUMMER FROM HELL

KABUL, 2007

I am a guest at an Afghan wedding in Kabul. Two hotel halls filled with guests. One for women, one for men. All the formalities happen in the women's hall. Rendered speechless by the power of the drum, I, like the rest of the men wait for the food.

"Are you enjoying the party?"
"Yes," I reply
But, in fact
I lie.

Blasting music. No one can speak
Decibels are in
Conversation's out
No one can hear me
even when I SHOUT.

And, so boring
All the men in one hall
The women in another
The only males the bride will see
are father, groom and brother.

While, in my room
filled with expressionless men.
Sensual youths dance, like women
How incongruent
But then
they won't see any females
until the signal comes
for the retreat
and at the door
they'll meet the wife, and daughters
and take them back
to domestic purdah.
This is the custom, this is the order.

The noise, the pain
My ears say STOP!
But the electronic drums are a hurtling train,
If I shout or scream,
no one will hear.
No help will come
from all those bored masks
silenced by that drum.

And the masks, stare into space
waiting, for the food
which never seems to come.

Everyone knows the truth
It's all too loud
But there we stare
glassy eyed, immobilised
captive sheep
glued to the crowd
and nothing can be done.

Is this what it's like to be in hell
To be there but not present
Alienated from the celebration
Excommunicated from all communication
Condemned to an eternity of loneliness
by the soul-destroying sounds
of the deceiving drummer's spell.
For, the father of lies, has poisoned Adam's well
from whence my dehumanised humanity
springs and dwells.

Sometimes I'm the victim of darkness
And sometimes, from deep within
darkness I create.
Oh how I hate this fetteredness
Will I ever be freed, from the noise of sin?

But, wait!
Here comes the Cosmic Bridegroom,
offering the very best of wine.
Transforming it from water.
Joyfully he shouts:

For all, I have restored the well
Come sons
Come daughters
Come drink, and dine.

And listen!
Listen
The drummer from hell
has gone.

Only a drum is pleased by its own sound.
AFGHAN PROVERB

SIXTY-SEVEN

THE CIGARETTE

KABUL, 2008

The noose of unemployment is tightening around the necks of hundreds of waiting men at the Khote Sangi roundabout.

And Wali has chosen his next victim.

Wali's name means "saint", but he is no saint. His smart clothes look out of place among the crowd of faded *shalwar kamiz*. He's not out of place though; he's right where he wants to be. He builds up a relationship over a few days, or a few weeks if need be. The desperate eyes will resist at first, but they usually give in.

They will blame the government. Blame the Americans. Blame the rich. Blame the bribe-takers. Perhaps they are right, but that is not Wali's concern. He will agree with them. He will fuel their desperation, reinforce their vulnerability and stoke their anger. It all helps to ripen the fruit. And there is plenty of fruit to be picked in the big roundabout at Khote Sangi.

He lights a cigarette and moves toward his target in the crowd of hungry men.

"*As salaam alekoom*, Shahzar, my brother." They share the customary embrace. Shahzar's fingers feel a layer of fat while the Saint's feel nothing but bony ribs. "My dear friend, you are so thin these days, and you look so tired. How long have you been standing here in this mob?"

Shahzar grits his teeth. "Since daybreak. You have to be here before dawn to get a good position."

Wali flashes his gold wristwatch. "And here it is seven hours later, and you are still here, my brother?"

An empty truck pulls up on the other side of the huge roundabout. Shahzar knows it is futile to rush across there. He would lose his first row position on this side. Sure enough, four men with shovels are quickly selected. The turbaned foreman in the grubby *shalwar* reaches down and drags the lucky quartet onto the tray, shouting to the driver, "*Booro, booro!* Go, go!"

Shovel in hand, a thin man springs from the crowd and leaps upward. A boot planted squarely between his eyes thrusts him backwards into the dirt.

Wali shakes his head. "Foolish man! They only wanted four, and only Hazaras. Not Pashtuns." He turns and extends a hand toward Shahzar. "Have a cigarette, my friend."

Shahzar hesitates. He stopped smoking six months ago. No money, no smoking. He only gets chosen for a day job about once a week. But early every morning, he brings his trowel and mason's hammer in a hessian bag. He sleeps on them for a while after midday when few employers come.

Wali moves his other hand, allowing the smoke to drift upwards into his victim's nostrils. Slowly the mason reaches for the addictive weed and lights up from Wali's flickering lighter. He draws deeply. It's an angry draw, and he hates himself for taking it.

He knows who Wali is. He knows the smart, neatly pressed outfit represents money. Drug money. And he knows why Wali is here. They both come from the same province, and Wali's boss is having some trouble moving his products. The authorities need to be sent a message: "Back off! Leave the roads alone at night!" A few roadside bombs should do it. A highway near Shahzar's ancestral village has been chosen.

"We'll supply the gear," Wali has repeatedly told him. "Everyone knows you; they won't suspect a thing. Just tell them you're back to visit your uncles."

Shahzar takes another angry drag.

Why can't this government do more? Billions of dollars have poured into this country. Why aren't there more jobs? And it's going to get worse as the foreign troops pull out. But the big mansions still go up. Those big shots aren't going to miss out. Get it while you can. Move the opium. Bribe your way into the lucrative contracts. Make sure your sons and nephews find their way into the government jobs to take money from us little people. Little people like Bahram, who had to sell his daughter to pay the fat landlord for back rent.

And then there are the local support troops the government has set up. Supposed to protect their village from the Taliban, because they are locals and they know who is who. They know who is who all right. They know when to knock down doors and rape the girls. And no one can touch them with their AK47s and army fatigues.

And what can the new President do? It took them months to fight out who stuffed the ballot boxes the most. Sure, he will start off well. They all do. But he owes a lot of favours. He says he'll get the mining going. Says we've got copper, iron, oil and gas. But who is brave enough to take it out while the Taliban are hovering around?

Wali gives a quiet cough. "Have you thought about it, my friend? I will pay you something in advance, you know. Your family will be pleased to see a decent meal for a change."

Shahzar says nothing. *How long can I go back empty handed to those ten hungry eyes? It's a man's responsibility to provide.* The gimlet of humiliation twists deeper in his gut. He's borrowed as much as he can from his brother, and the shopkeepers are demanding payment. He doesn't look his wife in the eye these days. He is too ashamed. "Your family named you Shahzar, King of Gold—" she exploded one foodless night. She never finished the sentence, and she doesn't complain any more, because he struck her across the face with his full force. "The Quran says a man can discipline his wife if he has to."

But he is still ashamed. Ashamed that he took out his anger on her. If it wasn't for the embroidery she did all day to sell to that foreign woman, they would be worse off.

Shahzar stubs the last vestige of the cigarette into the ground. Grinds it hard under his heel. "What do I have to do?" he says.

Wali smiles.

No one has ever become poor by giving.
ANNE FRANK

SIXTY-EIGHT

GROUNDED

ADELAIDE, 2008

Our doctor closed my ophthalmologist's report and leaned across her desk.
"Grant, it's clear that you can't go back to Afghanistan. There's nothing we can do for your eyesight. Soon you won't be able to drive or read. And, Janna, it's time for you to take a break from all that accumulating stress."
I was the director of Afghanistan's biggest eye-care program. I worked with international donors, Members of Parliament, Afghanistan's Ministry of Health, and a great team of dedicated people, both Afghans and expats. I flew to the four points of the country visiting eye hospitals, clinics and training centres. But none of them could help me now.
I looked at my gutsy wife.
All those stressful times when I was away.
Masked men peering in through the windows.
Nine-year-old Matthew vibrating, hair standing on end, fingers grasping a faulty socket.
Her best friend, killed on the road. Another blown up. Another poisoned.
Colleagues kidnapped. Some didn't come back.
Driving through narrow mountain passes, with me curled up sick on the back seat.
Her hepatitis, not once, but twice.
Distant children. Useless phone.
Angela, delirious with malaria.
That faulty diagnosis for Maria. "Nothing can be done for your knees. By the time you are twenty-one, you will be in a wheelchair."

Her compassion poured out on widows and raggedy girls—her "uncut diamonds and hidden pearls".

Desert cobras. Stinging scorpions.

Expelled from Pakistan without reason.

Sand and snow. Dust and rain.

And the constant strain of living in Taliban territory.

I could go on.

All those years she stood by me.

I remember the unofficial feedback from one of our cross-cultural trainers before we left Australia: "I doubt she will last long out there." Well, after sharing twenty-four years together on the field, there is no argument about her stickability. It was like the time her high school principal patted her on the shoulder and said, "My dear, the world needs shop assistants." With prayer and perseverance, the potential shop assistant followed her passion to be a teacher. And that same formula—passion, perseverance and prayer—plus some revolutionary, hold-your-breath therapy, made her a blessing from the sands of the Sindh to the streets of Kabul.

There is a lot of interest in the Islamic world at present. With Islamic State now outdoing the Taliban and al-Qaeda, people want to know what Islam is like on the ground. They want to know how to relate to our Australian Muslims. We receive many invitations to speak, and I continue writing with my talking computer programs.

※

On our nicely paved Australian roads, and in our well-stocked, impersonal supermarkets, Janna often feels out of place. She misses the face-to-face bargaining in Kabul's bustling bazaars. But one thing she never misses is tip-toeing around the buzzing mounds of maggoty rubbish expanding into the streets.

Every Monday morning, when that diesel truck roars up and clunk-clunks our bins into its cavernous body, Janna still rushes to the window to lay eyes on her hero.

Yes, she is still in love with the garbage man.

And so am I.

SIXTY-NINE

FLOTSAM

ADELAIDE, 2008

Sometimes I feel
like a ship
without an anchor
flotsam on the sea
flower without a petal
leaf without a tree.

And sometimes I feel
like a spoon
without a handle
a shoe without a lace
a wick without a candle
a human without a race.

But when all is done and said
I run to the one
who gives out the bread
and the jam and the cream
along with the thorns
and the eternal dream.

Till the sands run dry
at the end of time
I know His name
and He knows mine.

Crisp, beautiful and revealing. Valuable for anyone trying to build an appreciation of Islamic societies. And that should be all of us.

John Anderson
Former Deputy Prime Minister of Australia

Lock's adventures are probed for meaning so that the reader may have a deeper comprehension of a region frequently in our headlines but seldom in our understanding.

Lynn Arnold
Former Premier of South Australia

The raw reality of daily life for ordinary people, up close and personal. Lock gives the most pressing global issues of our time a human face.

Mark Durie
Author of *The Third Choice*

Your book brought back so many memories. I couldn't help but cry.

Habiba
Afghan refugee

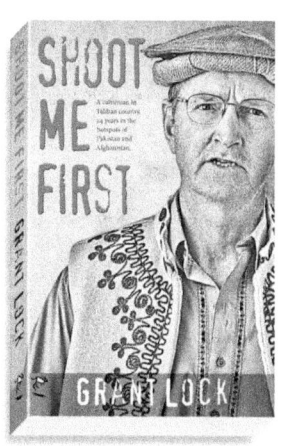

 **Shoot Me First**

Paperback. Audiobook. eBook

www.ingramcontent.com/pod-product-compliance
Lightning Source LLC
Chambersburg PA
CBHW051119160426
43195CB00014B/2262